BOAT MODELLING

V. E. Smeed

An introduction to the fast growing hobby of model boating by an author who has proved his versatility by a number of successful designs covering most types of model and has wide experience of the most frequent difficulties confronting the newcomer through the medium of readers' queries to 'Model Maker and Model Boats' of which he is Editor.

Model and Allied Publications Ltd

13–35 Bridge Street, Hemel Hempstead, Hertfordshire, England

Model and Allied Publications Limited
Book Division, Station Road,
Kings Langley, Hertfordshire

First Published	1956
Second Impression	1956
Third Impression	1957
Fourth Impression	1958
Fifth Impression	1960
Sixth Impression	1962
Seventh Impression	1964
Eighth Impression	1966
Ninth Impression	1968
Tenth Impression	1969
Eleventh Impression	1970
Twelfth Impression	1972
Thirteenth Impression	1973

ISBN 0 85344 066 2

*Reproduced and printed by photolithography and bound in
Great Britain at The Pitman Press, Bath*

Contents

Introduction

This book sets out to cover the whole subject of present-day model boating in as comprehensive a manner as possible. Naturally, in attempting to embrace every aspect of so vast a subject in one small volume, some items must inevitably suffer by abbreviation, and, in looking through what has been written, I cannot see one single subject on which I would not like to have written more! However, in every case the important points are covered and the best or most popular method of construction is given if there is insufficient space to detail several methods. Yachting enthusiasts will, I fear, feel that too much space is devoted to power boats—it is little comfort to consider that power boat fans will undoubtedly feel the reverse!

Model Boats can justly claim to be the oldest of all working models, and have developed through the centuries until nowadays their design, construction, and operation are frequently held to be a science. Science, of course, is nothing more than organised common sense, and I have therefore stressed the practical side of the hobby in this book, bearing in mind that each month sees new faces at the waterside. If the book helps those new faces to become familiar to existing enthusiasts, its primary object will be achieved.

V. E. SMEED

Chapter One
A Look at the Subject

THE expression "model boats" covers an astonishingly wide field. On the one hand are the small power craft and yachts seen at almost any time in the hands of youthful owners at the local park pondside, and on the other are the enthusiasts' highly efficient racing machines and the research models which contribute so much to technical advances in the full-size world. Between these extremes lies a fascinating selection of classes—so many that it is perhaps advisable to group them as conveniently as possible at the outset of this book.

Power Craft

There are various forms of power plant in common use, and various types of boats to use them; practically any combination can be used, so let us first examine the available means of power.

(i) Rubber—a somewhat neglected propulsive force, yet one which is inexpensive, simple to operate, and capable of giving excellent performance.

(ii) Clockwork—still the chief motive power of toy boats but, in the form of converted clock or gramophone motors, not to be despised by the serious modeller.

(iii) Electric motors—widely favoured in all types of model where high speeds are not required. Clean, cool, quiet, and uncomplicated, excellent for speed control, etc. Disadvantages are weight and space requirements for batteries or accumulators, and relatively high operating costs (q.v.).

(iv) Petrol engines—excellent for many models unless reversing is required, when a relatively complicated clutch is called for. Good speed control, fairly simple operation provided the ignition system is thoroughly water-proof.

(v) Glowplug engines—at one time these were only used where the last ounce of performance was required; now fitted in many boats, but careful protection of the structure against fuel is necessary.

(vi) Diesel engines—more correctly expressed as "compression ignition" engines; these have done much to bring about the recent tremendous increase in model power boat popularity. Straightforward to instal and operate, but speed control is limited and steps must be taken against fuel soakage.

(vii) Steam plants—still enjoy a certain popularity though a little bulky and heavy for the power produced. Flash steam and advanced engines are used even in hydroplanes; heat and "mess" a disadvantage for radio control.

(viii) Jetex motors—suitable for special models only, but quite simple to fit and operate.

(ix) Jet motors—have little application in model boats and few examples have been seen.

Types of Boats

It is rather difficult to draw an exact line between some classes of models, but the following list embraces the entire range in general terms.

(i) Sport models—usually semi-scale in appearance but simple in construction, may be powered by any of the above forms of propulsion. Size varies from a few inches to five or six feet, but two to three feet overall is most popular.

(ii) Semi-scale models—the definition of "semi-scale" is normally a model which, if scaled up, could conceivably be a seaworthy full-size craft. The expression "near-scale" is usually applied to a model based on a prototype but usually simplified. Such models constitute the great majority of the small craft afloat today, and can resemble any type of vessel from launches to liners or warships. Most forms of power apply.

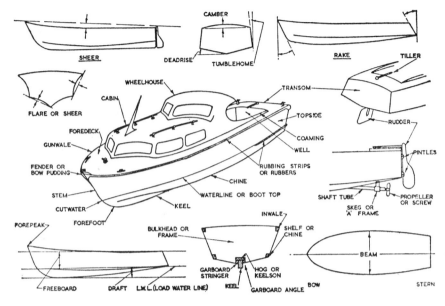

(iii) Scale models—may be accurate representations of any size of virtually anything afloat. Electric power is most frequently used, except for fast launch types, when diesels predominate.

(iv) Steering models—used in competitions, these are frequently specially designed to maintain straight, predetermined courses, and include reasonable draught with large underwater fins and little side area above water-level. Most forms of power are suitable, but accurate speed control is an advantage. Length is usually three to four feet.

(v) Airscrew-driven hydroplanes—frequently simple models, and popular because no complicated drive is involved. Usually fitted with diesel motors, fast and exciting to operate; the European record is well over 100 m.p.h.

(vi) Hydroplanes—a specialised branch of model boats, rarely using anything but i.c. engines and usually run tethered. Fast and exciting, but requiring skill.

(vii) Special models—submarines, auxiliary sailing vessels, and unorthodox models generally. Operated for sport or experimentation.

(viii) Radio-controlled models—these can be of almost any of the foregoing types, provided that sufficient room is available for the necessary equipment, but far and away the most popular are the semi-scale hard chine launch types of 30-40 ins. length.

Sailing Craft

Most sailing models nowadays are Bermuda rig racing yachts, and there are six official classes built to special rules (see appendices). In order of size, these are as follows :

"A" CLASS.

Built to a special formula, "A" boats are normally between 6 and 7 ft. long and between 50 and 70 lb. displacement, with a mast up to 8 ft. in length carrying a sail area averaging around 1,650 sq. in.

12 METRE.

Scaled at 1 in. to 1 ft. from full-size craft, giving a length of around 70 in., this class is now virtually non-existent.

10 RATERS.

These boats are also built to a special rule and approximate 6 ft. in length, weigh somewhere between 25 and 30 lb., and carry a sail area of roughly 1,100 sq. in.

6 METRE.

These boats are the nearest approach to scale model yachts but because of the complicated rule are no longer very popular. Length is normally a little over 5 ft., displacement in the order of 32 or 33 lb., plus a crew weight of 2 lb., carrying somewhere between 1,100 and 1,200 sq. in. of sail.

MARBLEHEAD.

Of American origin, Marbleheads are built to the simplest specification, the main features of which are a maximum length of 50 in., and a maximum sail area of 800 sq. in. Displacement is normally between 20 and 24 lb.

36 in. RESTRICTED.

The smallest recognised class, the basic rules being that the hull must fit into a box 36 x 9 x 11 with a maximum displacement of 12 lb. Sail area is unlimited.

Three of these classes are recognised internationally, the "A" class, the 6 metre, and the Marblehead; the last mentioned is probably the most popular class of model yacht at present in existence.

Yacht builders are advised to contact their local clubs before finally deciding upon a design, since few clubs race every class of model, and there is little point in producing a class boat for which there is no local competition.

There is one popular unofficial class, this being the Half-Marblehead, ½M, or as it is normally known, MM Class. This was introduced by MODEL MAKER at the beginning of 1955, and is thus a relatively recent innovation; nevertheless, an enormous number of these models are being sailed. The primary aim was to encourage newcomers with a small and inexpensive *racing* design, and the chief rules are an overall length limited to 25 in., and a maximum sail area of 216 sq. in. The full rating is set out in Appendix II.

Naturally, sport models are found in the world of sail, but the modern trend is to build class boats even for pleasure sailing, or to break right away from the Bermuda rig and build semi-scale or scale models of schooners, yawls, barges, and even square-rig vessels. The size of such models is again a question of the builder's taste, and may vary from a few inches to several feet.

The only remaining class of sailing model is the radio-controlled yacht; the Model Yachting Association recognises all vane class for radio sailing, with the prefix R—RA, R10r, R6m, RM, and R36r. Of these by far the most popular is the RM, where a total radio weight of up to 2 lbs. is customary. Control systems are mentioned in Chap. 15.

Competitions

A very diverse range of competitions have become standardised for model power boats, and there is no doubt that such contests add considerably to the pleasure given by the hobby. Most builders eventually reach the stage of wanting to compare their models' performances with those of other enthusiasts, and this is made easy even for the lone hand by the natural friendliness and the spirit of good-natured rivalry common to all boat fans. More can be learned by attendance at one competition than in twelve months' work on one's

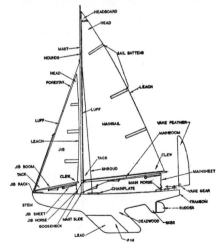

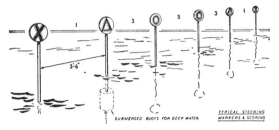

FIG. 3 (left): Markers for steering competitions are mounted on sticks or carried on buoys.

FIG. 4 (below): A typical course for radio control steering events.

own, and a large number of clubs exist throughout the British Isles, all of which run competition programmes throughout the year. Even if you can only get along to three or four meetings a year, joining an established club is well worthwhile; a list of clubs will be found in Appendix III and V.

The normal competitions for model power boats are:

(i) Nomination event—this is usually limited to boats with speeds of less than 12 m.p.h., and consists of a straight run over a course of 50 or 80 yards. The competitor has to nominate the time his boat will take to cover the course, and, naturally, the boat with the smallest error wins. Success in this calls for a reliable boat capable of steering a straight course, and with machinery which can be confidently reset at the same r.p.m. at any time, plus, of course, the ability to estimate wind effect, etc., which comes with practice.

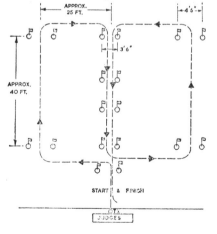

(ii) Steering event—in this, the boat covers a course of 50 or 80 yds. towards a set of markers spaced $3\frac{1}{2}$ ft. apart. Scoring is 1, 3, 5, 3, and 1 (Fig. 3). The same model requirements as above apply.

(iii) Speed events—these are run with the models tethered to a central pylon. Line lengths and strengths, model classes, and speed records are given in the appendices, but it may be mentioned here that these events are virtually entirely given over to hydroplanes.

(iv) Radio control steering event—here the models are required to steer between pairs of buoys set out in a course as in Fig. 4. Points are scored for passing between each pair of buoys, with smaller scores for missing on the inside or outside, depending on the position of the buoys in relation to the course. In addition some of these competitions include points for demonstrating "special effects" and speed control, after the course has been completed. The competition may also be broken down into sections segregating the various motive powers or the varying degree of control fitted, i.e. rudder-only boats may be separate from those having rudder, engine speed, reversing, and other controls.

(v) Radio control speed runs—usually a triangular or figure-8 course, with no real steering hazards. Three classes of i.c. engined boats and two electric classes are recognised—0-2$\frac{1}{2}$, 2$\frac{1}{2}$-5, and 5-30 c.c., and up to 30 and 300 watt.

Sailing Competitions

There are few variations in competitions for sailing craft, all of which are races.

(i) Races on lakes, etc., are overwhelmingly the most common. The "American tournament" system is employed, i.e. boats are raced two at a time, but every boat meets every other entrant. Each pair make a beat to windward (into the wind) for which the winner receives 3 points, and a run to leeward (downwind) for which the winner receives 2 points. A complete race by one pair (once up and once down the lake) is termed a "heat" and a complete series between all pairs a "round".

(ii) Races on open water—these are very infrequent and are difficult due to the speed of modern yachts. Each competitor sails his model round a triangular course, using a dinghy to re-trim. As many boats may perform as can be conveniently sailed.

(iii) Radio control races—rules are based on full-size yacht racing rules; yachts sail round a triangular or rectangular course and may not be handled or touched after starting. Superhet radio equipment is necessary to sail boats together without radio interference; normally boats sail in pairs but up to twelve or fifteen take part in occasional mass races. Lighter, improved radio equipment is attracting more people to this type of sailing, which takes considerable skill.

Organising Bodies

There are two main controlling bodies covering all model boat activity in this country, the Model Yachting Association, which deals with sailing craft, and the Model Power Boat Association, which governs power models, racing hydroplanes, etc. The work put in by these bodies is entirely on a voluntary basis and the amount of work done is of considerable value to all enthusiasts, although it may not always be evident.

Apart from formulating regulations and carrying out other committee business, both the governing bodies organise a full annual programme of meetings, which are distributed geographically in order that the difficulties of travelling are shared by enthusiasts in various parts of the country. As an example of this, the premier yachting event of the year is the British and Open A Class Championships, which lasts for a week, and is held in the north of England one year and in the south the next.

Naturally, the authority of the central bodies is broken down over a wide area by means of numerous clubs who affiliate to their respective parent organisation. Members of affiliated clubs enjoy the benefits obtained for them by the hard work of their officials—benefits which range from the use of stretches of water to comprehensive insurance, etc.—and are of course able to participate in official events without difficulty. In the case of yacht clubs, where the models are built to strict specifications, each club is equipped with a measuring tank and has an official measurer who fills in a rating certificate for each new model. Without a rating certificate the model has no official sail number and cannot enter into official races. Similar functions are carried out by power boat officials.

"Lone hand" modellers are recommended to get in touch with their nearest club, where, for what is normally a nominal subscription, they may share in the advantages of organised activity. If, however, you live in an isolated locality and operate entirely alone, it may still be an advantage to join a club as an inexpensive way of obtaining insurance, etc., though, in fact, many insurance companies will offer third party cover for an individual for a very nominal sum. Most local councils insist on such insurance cover for modellers operating boats on their waters, the cover being usually £50,000 minimum.

Chapter Two

Tools and Materials

THE number of tools required to build a model boat will vary considerably with the individual as well as with the type of model under construction. For this reason the following are lists of more or less minimum requirements—some builders will, no doubt, make do without some items, while others will be able to work better with additional tools not mentioned here.

For the average, simple hard chine launch type, the following are suggested. (1) Small tenon saw—there is an excellent 7 in. saw with a hand-brush type of handle available cheaply in multiple stores. (2) Junior hacksaw (Eclipse) for both wood and metal cutting. (3) Fret saw. (4) Small plane. (5) ½ in. chisel. (6) Light hammer. (7) One or two screwdrivers. (8) Hand-drill, three or four assorted drills, and a rose countersink. (9) Pliers, preferably taper-nose. (10) One or two small G-cramps. (11) Try-square. (12) Sharp knife or single-edged razor blades.

No more tools than this are required for planked hulls, although a marking gauge is handy if you are used to using one, and one or two files, and even a rasp, may save a lot of glass-papering. Carved hulls get a bit more towards the real carpentry outfit, and besides the above list it is useful to have:

(13) Assorted chisels. (14) Assorted gouges—two or three different sizes are enough. (15) Spoon gouge, about ¾ in. (16) Carpenter's brace and assorted bits, especially a 1 in. size. (17) Calipers. (18) Spokeshave.

For large models, a bow-saw and a jack-plane are helpful, but most builders will be able to assess their requirements when studying plans for the proposed model. A useful tool is an Abrafile, which will cut in any direction, and is used mounted in a hacksaw frame. Other handy gadgets can be made in the workshop; one example is the simple cramp in Fig. 6. This is made up from two lengths of studding (screwed rod) to which are fitted two strips of wood adjusted up and down by nuts, preferably wing-nuts. Several of these cramps will be needed for a bread-and-butter hull.

Needless to say, all pins, nails, or screws which will remain part of the structure must be rustless; brass is the normal material for these, though some very fine pins are made only in copper. The most useful type of brass pin is known as a "gimp" pin, and is available in sizes from ¼ in. up, and it has a flat head of nearly $\frac{1}{16}$ in. diameter, and is thus not so prone to pulling through as brass veneer or panel pins. Screws used are normally those with countersunk heads, and when a screw is driven in, it pays to follow the correct method by drilling a clearance hole for the shank and a thread hole to provide adequate bite for the thread without the risk of splitting the work.

A wide variety of glues now exists, and for boat-building there are several specialised products. The first essential is insolubility in water, which rules out such things as Scotch or other animal glues. Some cellulose cements are excellent, especially for work with balsa; harder woods need the slow-drying cements such as "Britfix" or "Durofix".

Unquestionably the best results are obtained with the comparatively recent resin glues. Some of these (Aerolite, Beetle, etc.), are two-part mixes—the resin is applied to one surface and a hardener to the other. The glue commences to cure when the surfaces are brought together, but a short time is available for positioning the joint ac-

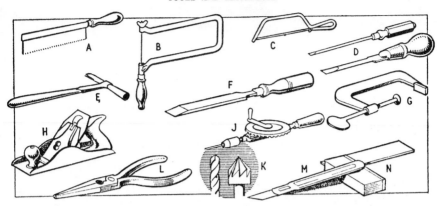

curately. Setting time is affected by temperature, but on average is in the order of 4-6 hours. One resin glue (Cascamite One-Shot) is sold in powder form, ready-mixed and requiring only the addition of water to be ready to use. All these glues are completely water- and heat-proof when set, and they all have the advantage of being gap-filling. This means that when two slightly irregular surfaces are glued, no air-space will remain, since any discrepancies will be filled by the glue. Although the advantages of this are apparent, and the strength of resin glues is enormous, it should not be made an excuse for sloppy workmanship—a top-line boat calls for complete accuracy from start to finish.

Only best quality paints and varnishes should be used if a reasonable finish and life expectancy is required. A few coppers saved here can spoil the best model, and this includes brushes too. There are several good paints suitable for the purpose, but if possible marine paints should be used. Cellulose is not really suitable, since it tends to sit on the surface and although hard is prone to abrade, or, if water does find its way behind it, blister off. Lead paints are good if an annual re-paint is envisaged, but for general ease of working, good finish, and excellent life, modern synthetics are to be preferred. It is a little invidious to single out one of several good products for special mention, but because of its availability anywhere a

recommendation can be made—when in doubt use "Valspar". A later chapter deals with painting and gives full information on this subject.

Finally, to the all-important subject of timber. Builders of hard chine or diagonal-planked hulls are fortunate, for the most reliable timber of all is resin-bonded birch ply, and it is readily available in all sizes from $\frac{1}{32}$ in. up. Occasionally, this may only be found in metric sizes, but the range of sizes is virtually identical and it is close enough to work on the basis of 3 mm. = $\frac{1}{8}$ in.

Where timber is required in plank

FIG. 5 (above) shows the normal tools required for a simple boat. Carved hulls are easier with the addition of the extra tools illustrated below.

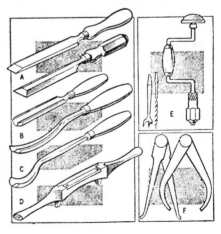

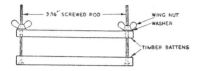

FIG. 6.—Cramp for bread and butter hulls.

form, the position is by no means so happy. You may be lucky in finding a local yard able to supply suitable wood, but nowadays timber is very frequently kiln-dried, and in nine cases out of ten what may look to be excellent material for the job will eventually let you down. For bread-and-butter hulls the amount of "movement" (from drying out or from residual stresses produced by kiln-drying) is not likely to be serious, but for a planked hull the results can be disastrous. If you cannot buy guaranteed timber locally, send away to one of the model suppliers who can make a special selection through a timber importer ; it may cost you a shilling or two more, but is well worth it in the long run.

An alternative and possibly even better scheme is to have a look round sale-rooms and so on, for an old piece of furniture or a door which you can have cut at a sawyers. Timber obtained from such a source is often ideal for planking and laminated keels ($\frac{3}{4}$ in. is the normal maximum width for such items). The timbers best suited to model work are Douglas Fir, Silver Spruce, Yellow Pine, Red Cedar, Hickory, Maple, African Whitewood, and, of course, Mahogany (preferably American). Of these, cedar, yellow pine and mahogany are outstand-

ing, and these woods can occasionally be found at yards dealing in "reconditioned" timber. The most easily available "new" timber, not in the foregoing list, is Obeche (sometimes "obechi"), and if thoroughly dried, etc., this is quite suitable for bread-and-butter hulls. It has the added advantages of being easy to work, and, in normal cases, light in weight, so that a hull need not be carved out quite as thin as is sometimes necessary.

Boat-building sizes differ from normal timber sizes for prepared (planed all round) wood. Customarily 1 in. x 2 in. timber refers to the "sawn" size, and the dimensions are nominal for planed material, which should be $\frac{1}{8}$ in. under-size, i.e. $\frac{7}{8}$ in. x $1\frac{7}{8}$ in. in this example. Sizes given in boat-building are finished sizes, i.e. actual sizes after planing. This is important, particularly when working to a lines drawing for bread-and-butter construction, so if you are having timber sawn and prepared for you, be very specific. Many experts have their planks left $\frac{1}{32}$ in. oversize and plane down to exact size by hand. To ensure constant thickness over several planks, ask for them to be fed through a thicknesser rather than processed on an overhand planer.

In the foregoing, we have assumed average facilities for intending builders. Obviously, a bench and a carpenter's vice are assets, and some modellers may have power tools at their disposal. However, there is no need to be discouraged if your equipment is limited—a good many championship models have been built on no more than the humble kitchen table!

Chapter Three Hard Chine Hulls

A HARD chine hull is one in which the sides and bottom join to produce an angle, rather than merging gently from one to the other in a curve. The continuous angle, running from near the bow to the stern, is the chine line, and "hard" in this sense is an old shipwright's expression which, for definitive purposes, can be taken as "acute". Hard chine hulls are also known as "sharpies" or, simply, "chine boats".

The beauty of the hard chine is its extreme simplicity and speed in construction, coupled with a smaller outlay in money and skill. Little use of the idea is made in the full-size industry for boats of over 120 ft. or so in length (although one enterprising firm is now producing flat-bottomed craft with "sharp corners") since there are certain disadvantages in stability and strength/weight ratio in really big sizes ; however, for modelling the advantages far outweigh any disadvantages.

When a boat is placed in the water, it will displace a volume of water corresponding to its total weight (remember Archimedes?). In actual fact, and as a point of interest, 1.8 cu. in. of water weighs one ounce, so that for example a 5 lb. boat will displace 80 x 1.8 or 144 cu. in. of water. Now, this water is continually displaced as the boat moves along, even at maximum normal speed. If, however, the boat is overdriven, i.e. more power is applied than is needed to maintain maximum normal speed, the boat, by virtue of its shape (without go-

ing into a lot of theory) will tend to rise out of the water and begin to "plane", that is, sit on its stern with its bow out of the water. Part of the boat's weight is transferred to the air and the harder the boat is driven the greater is the proportion of weight transferred. The maximum speed of the boat in this condition is considerably higher, of course.

Now, a boat deliberately designed to achieve high speeds above any other considerations, must be designed to plane, and a planing boat requires light weight, a flat run (Fig. 8) and a relatively broad transom or stern end, since this is where it will be chiefly supported by the water at speed. The hard chine hull is ideal for these conditions, which is why air/sea rescue launches, motor torpedo boats, and other fast craft employ this system.

The disadvantages of the hard chine are more apparent in sailing craft. Given sufficient wind, yachts will plane on the run, but working across or into the wind (reaching or beating) calls for hull characteristics in which the chine hull does not noticeably shine ; chief among these is the necessity to sail at a slight heel (the "sailing angle") and chine boats prefer to be sailed upright. Even so, the principle reason for the absence of hard chine hulls in full-size sailing is that the rules frequently preclude them ; there are, of course, special classes (e.g. "Star"

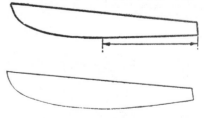

FIG. 7 (left) shows a typical hard chine cross-section. FIG. 8 (right) contrasts a flat run with a more curved profile.

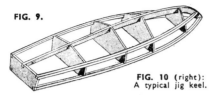

FIG. 9.

FIG. 10 (right):
A typical jig keel.

and "Cadet") which are for chine boats only. On the model side, the windward work of sharpies puts them slightly at a disadvantage, although such boats have finished in the top half-dozen in more than one national competition.

It will thus be seen that the hard chine is excellent for power boats, where constant power is available irrespective of the wind, but has limitations for sailing craft. For a beginner, the simplicity of construction frequently outweighs any limitations in performance, so that whether power or sail is preferred, a boat with this type of hull should be first choice for a novice.

Construction

The basic hull of a sharpie at its simplest consists of five longitudinal members—a central keel, two chines (sometimes called "chine stringer" or "shelf") and two inwales (Fig 9) to form the remaining two corners of a pentagon —plus a number of lateral members ("frames" or "bulkheads") and a stem and stern. There are two methods of producing this basic assembly (a) by making the keel member a jig to which the bulkheads are fitted, or (b) by erecting the bulkheads in a separate jig (upside down), and adding the keel, chines, and inwales, removing the jig at a later stage in the building schedule. Which of these two basic methods is adopted depends on whether the bulkheads are to remain a permanent part of the finished hull.

The average power boat is built up as a complete structure, with all the components added during building remaining part of the finished model. Usually this means a fairly generous keel member upon which the bulkheads can be fitted

and aligned positively, but occasionally "egg-box" construction is used (Fig. 12). In this, two longitudinal built-in jigs receive the bulkheads, each item being slotted so that positive alignment is assured. Light inwales, chines, and keel are added before planking or skinning. An advantage of this system is that an accurate hull can be built by anyone able to wield a saw reasonably well. With a single keel care must be taken when fitting inwales and chines to avoid stresses likely to lead to an asymmetric hull, and it is best to fit these members in their respective pairs.

FIG. 13.—Laminated keel/stem structure.

Breaking the assembly into detail, let us examine the most popular form of power boat hull. The first item is the keel, and the modern scheme is to cut this from ply which, needless to say, has to be of the waterproof, resin-bonded type. At one time the keel and stem were fashioned in one piece from a grown crook, but with ply this is unnecessary, since the stem can be cut as part of the keel. Occasionally a laminated keel/stem is used, particularly where a gentle curve exists at the bow, and this is made from thin strips glued

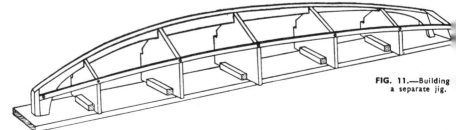

FIG. 11.—Building a separate jig.

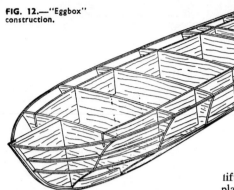

FIG. 12.—"Eggbox" construction.

together under pressure (see Fig. 13). Another method is to cut the stem and keel from timber of ⅜ in. thickness or more, making a glued joint reinforced by brass pins or screws and a "knee" cut from the same timber (Fig. 14).

With the normal single-screw boat, the propeller shaft must pass through the keel. There are two types of shaft, that which is enclosed in a tube for the whole of its length, and that which runs "in the open" and is provided only with a short "stuffing box" to provide a bearing and a seal where it enters the hull. The tube type has a bush at each end

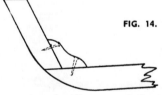

FIG. 14.

only, so that the diameter of the tube is rather greater than the shaft diameter; as an example, a ₁₆ⁿ in. shaft is normally found in a ⅜ in. o.d. tube. Exposed shafts are usually fitted to racing designs or very fast boats where a universal joint is required, but for the average boat the full-length tube is quite satisfactory.

The problem of passing a ⅜ in. tube through a keel which may be only ⅛ in. thick is overcome by fitting blocks on either side (Fig. 15). A strip is cut out of the keel at exactly the right angle

and width for the shaft, and the two parts pinned accurately in place over the plan One block is now glued in place and left to dry thoroughly, following which the assembly may be lifted and the second block glued in place and pinned or screwed through to the other. This is a much more accurate system than endeavouring to drill or burn a hole through after assembly. The

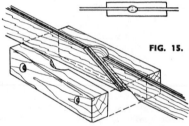

FIG. 15.

tunnel in the blocks may be drilled with the channel in the ply as a guide, but it is better to chisel and file each block before gluing in place. A close fit is not absolutely essential, since any gaps will later be filled with paint-soaked cotton waste rammed in tightly.

When a thick keel is used and it is necessary to drill a shaft tunnel (an operation usually performed at a late stage of assembly) much trouble can be avoided by making a simple jig as in Fig. 16. The length of hole to be drilled

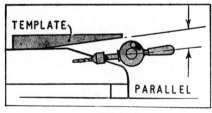

TEMPLATE

PARALLEL

FIG. 16.

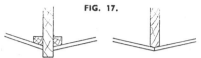

FIG. 17.

is usually considerably greater than that
of a standard drill, and unless a special
long-shanked auger bit is purchased it
is advisable to burn a pilot hole through
with a red-hot wire (about 12 s.w.g. is
adequate). This hole can then be followed from both ends and rat-tail file
used to finish the tunnel off.

It is usual for the keel assembly to
project slightly beneath the completed
boat, i.e. the planking or bottom skin
butts against the keel side. To assist
in making a good joint, some provision
is usually made for seating the skin, and
although the keel can be rebated for
this, it is much simpler to glue and pin
a stringer in place on each side of the
keel before assembly. These need only
be ⅛ in. square. On some designs the
bottom skin panels "overlap" the keel,
butting against each other to form a
smooth V along the whole length ; this
merely entails chamfering of the actual
keel to suit (Fig. 17).

The bulkheads or frames are glued in
place on the keel assembly (still considering the average model) and the
joints may be halved to ensure correct
positioning. Where a bulkhead is
simply notched to receive the keel,
skewed pins can be driven through to
strengthen the joint.

When all bulkheads and transom are
in position and dry, the inwales and

chines may be positioned. There is frequently a sharp curve towards the bow,
particularly with the inwales, and this
is sometimes sawn to shape from flat
material. Where a single strip is used,
it may be necessary to steam or soak
the curve in, and in this case it is advisable to pin or strap the strips in
place temporarily and allow them to dry
before gluing and pinning permanently.
Wetting tends to swell the wood and on
drying a contraction of ⅛ in. is quite to
be expected in a 3 ft. length ; this is
enough to pull the structure severely out
of shape. The best method is undoubtedly to laminate chines and inwales
from two or three more easily bent
strips, gluing along the whole length.
This also reduces splitting if pins are
driven through when attaching the skin.
When the glue is dry, plane off the strips
to their correct sections. If sufficiently
long strips of material are not available,
scarf two or more strips together, the
ideal joint line extending over a distance
of eight times the width of the material
(Fig. 18). Place such joints at points of
little stress, i.e. where the curve is slight.
When skinned, no difference in strength
will be noticeable.

The entire framework should now be
examined carefully for truth. Sight
along centre lines for symmetry, above
and below, and check that no twist has
crept in. Any internal details such as
motor mounts, etc., that must be fitted
before the hull is planked should be
attended to before proceeding further.

It is customary to "plank", "skin", or

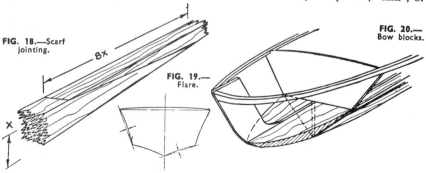

FIG. 18.—Scarf jointing.

FIG. 19.— Flare.

FIG. 20.— Bow blocks.

e yachts on the right belong to the largest
of models raced either nationally or internally, the A class. The two in the photo-
h are being released for a run and hence
spinnakers rigged. Displacement of such
boats averages 56 lb.

On the left are two 10-rater yachts about
to commence a run with spinnakers drawing
nicely. The boat nearer the camera is very
unusual in that it is a hard chine design, rare
in this class. The average 10-rater displacement is about 28 lb.

he most popular class of yacht is now the
n. Marblehead class, two examples of which
seen on the right drawing away from their
pers' hands on a beat to windward. Nor-
y about 22 lb. displacement, this type of
boat is relatively easy to transport.

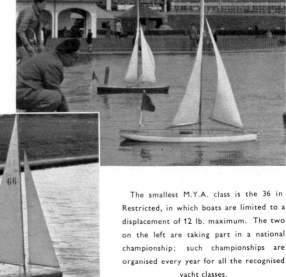

The smallest M.Y.A. class is the 36 in
Restricted, in which boats are limited to a
displacement of 12 lb. maximum. The two
on the left are taking part in a national
championship; such championships are
organised every year for all the recognised
yacht classes.

PLATE 1.

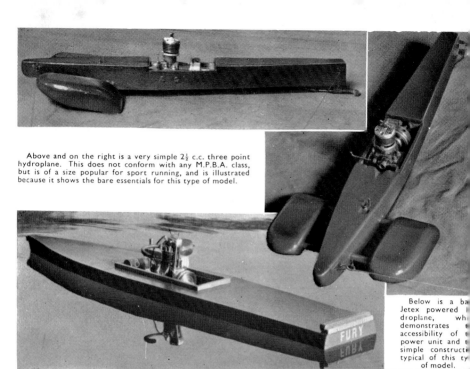

Above and on the right is a very simple 2½ c.c. three point
hydroplane. This does not conform with any M.P.B.A. class,
but is of a size popular for sport running, and is illustrated
because it shows the bare essentials for this type of model.

Below is a ba
Jetex powered
droplane, wh
demonstrates
accessibility of
power unit and
simple constructi
typical of this ty
of model.

Above is a steering
launch, which makes
no pretensions to
any scale appearance.
Power for this particu-
lar 48 in. model is a
10 c.c. o.h.v. petrol
engine, and the dis-
placement is 12 lb.

Left, a fine ex
ample of diagon
planking for a har
chine hull, photo
graphed befor
painting. The supe
structure of th
particular stea
launch is fabricate
entirely from dura
a job rather beyon
the scope of ar
but skilled met
workers.

The steam launch on the right is
shown nearing the end of its 80 yard
course to score an inner on the tar-
gets. The rules for steering contests
such as this may take the better of
two runs as the final score, or the
aggregate score of two or more runs.

PLATE 2.

"cover" the underside of the hull first, and the usual method is to cut thick brown paper or thin card templates to the approximate shape. The inner (garboard) edge is all that need be accurately fitted, and an overlap of about ¼ in. is all that need be left on the other edges. After the template is satisfactory, cut the ply and fit the garboard edge accurately by taking a fine shaving or two off with the plane to produce the slight chamfer necessary. Glue all the contacting surfaces, position the ply, and drive in pins, either as permanent fixtures, or to provide temporary pressure while the glue dries. In the latter case, hardened steel dressmakers' pins, pressed in at an angle with pliers, are ideal.

When the glue is thoroughly dry the

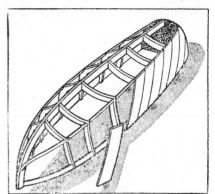

FIG. 22.—Diagonal planking.

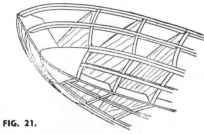

FIG. 21.

surplus material can be trimmed off with a sharp knife and the edges planed flush. The side skins can now be attached, allowing a small overlap all round, trimmed and planed off when dry.

Fitting the ply skins is not difficult except where sharp changes of angle are required or excessive sheer (concavity of the surface) occurs. In the former case the only really sharp change is at the boat's forefoot, and it is customary to fit solid blocks at this point (Fig. 20) or to plank the extreme bow with narrow vertical strips. Flare can usually be induced into ply by steaming or slight damping, or even leaving the cut sheet in a tray of wet sawdust for a few hours. In extreme cases narrow vertical strips can be used, and a sheer stringer let into the bulkheads midway between inwale and chine facilitates this (Fig. 21). Some-

times the extreme bow is built up from vertical strips of timber around ¼ in. thick, the flare being carved in when the glue is dry.

Some scale models may have flare running along the entire hull, sides and bottom. In such a case diagonal planking is frequently employed; this is a simple method and, if double diagonal planking is used, results in a remarkably strong hull. For most models the ply or timber can be cut into long strips 1 in. wide; the end of the strip is laid in place somewhere amidships, at an angle of 45° to the fore-and-aft line, marked off, and cut to length. A small overlap can remain if required. This strip is now glued and pinned in place (a sheer stringer running the length of the boat

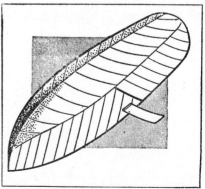

FIG. 23.—Double diagonal planking.

FIG. 24.

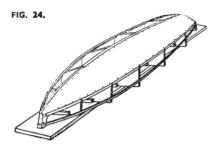

is desirable) and another strip laid up to it, cut, fitted, and so on, until the entire surface is planked. Double planking means laying on a second set of planks at right angles to the first. This system, using $\frac{1}{32}$ in. (.8 mm.) ply for each "layer", is excellent for strong, light hulls up to 48 in. in length.

Before decking, the interior of the hull requires painting (see Chap. IX). After painting and completion of internal detail, the deck, suitably cut for hatches, etc., can be glued and pinned in place, completing the basic hull.

A hard chine hull can, of course, be built without permanent bulkheads, and yachts with such hulls are usually built in this fashion. The "shadows" employed are more or less bulkheads which are later removed, and the essential difference in that the hull is built upside down on a jig in much the same manner as a planked hull. Reference to the next chapter will fill in the details of the following outline procedure.

The shadows are cut with sufficient material left above the inwale line to bring their top edges to a straight line. All required notches are cut for keel, chines, and inwales, and the shadows, stem, and transom are then erected on a jig board at their correct stations. The fore and aft members are added and lightly pinned in place (they can, of course, be glued to stem and transom) and the resulting frame skinned as previously detailed. Care must be taken to glue the skin only to the permanent structure. When dry, a rigid assembly remains, which can be cleaned up externally with complete safety. The assembly is then removed from the jig and the shadows twisted out. Timbering, deck beams, etc., can be added as each shadow is removed to reduce any chance of the hull springing out of shape.

The big advantages of hard chine hulls are that they are simple and quick to build, light in weight, and, of course, they offer little difficulty in timber supplies. Ply is the main material, and is reasonably easy to buy anywhere. The chines, etc., can be made from any long-grained wood, and spruce should be available in any respectable model or handicraft shop. Failing this, obeche can be used if no better choice lies to hand ; some of the exotic timbers imported—sanga, meranti, quaraba, etc., are perfectly suitable for such purposes, if thoroughly dry.

Chapter Four

Round Bilge Hulls

MOST full-size craft have "round bilge" hulls, the "bilge" being the part of the hull between the "floor" and the "side". When the floor curves gently into the side the hull is of the round bilge type ; softening the turn of the bilge means making the curve flatter, and hardening the turn is the reverse, terminating, of course, in the "hard chine" when a definite chine or corner exists.

A very high proportion of model boats do, of course, follow full-size prototypes to a greater or lesser extent, which means that the round-bilge hull is common in the model world. Most model yachts employ a rounded hull, too, since there are hydrodynamic advantages in this shape. At one time it was normal to carve such a hull out of one solid lump of timber, and for small hulls this may still be done (Fig. 26 gives the easiest system). However, the two main systems used nowadays are much easier and more economical ; these are the bread-and-butter and rib-and-plank methods.

Bread and Butter

In this system the bread is the timber and the butter the glue used to bond the planks together. There are two separate methods, bread and buttering on the waterlines, and bread and buttering on the buttocks. To explain these we must look at a typical lines drawings

of a hull as prepared by a naval architect ; a small scale reproduction is shown in Fig. 27. Looking at the profile of the hull, it will be seen that the shape is divided into equal "slices" by horizontal lines. These are the waterlines, and they are shown in full on the plan view of the hull just below. If timber of the same thickness as the "slices" is cut into a number of planks, each shaped to one of the waterlines, an embryo hull is immediately achieved. It will be apparent that all but the bottom plank can have much of the centre removed before assembly ; an accurate assessment of the required inner line can be made by sketching the structure and wall thickness over the body plan (the third part of the drawing) as in Fig. 29. If this is done on each section shown on the body plan, a series of points can be marked on the planks which when connected will give an inner line to saw to. Lower planks can frequently be cut from the inner parts of the upper planks to economise on materials.

The second method also uses the lines given on the drawing, in this case the parallel fore-and-aft lines dividing the plan view. These buttock lines are shown in full as the curved lines on the profile, and the planks will, of course, be vertical and in pairs. The same system of determining how much may be safely cut out can be followed. This

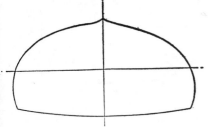

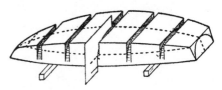

FIG. 25 (left) shows a typical round-bilge cross-section. FIG. 26 (above) preparing a block for carving.

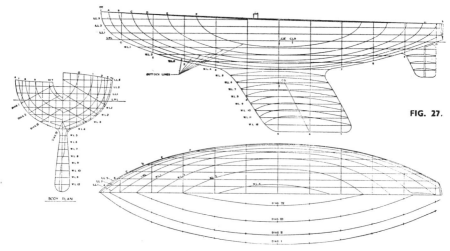

FIG. 27.

method has achieved considerable popularity in recent years, particularly for racing yachts. One special advantage is that it is easy to check that both sides are absolutely identical, since the joint lines can be used to ensure symmetry; this is of paramount importance.

Whichever method is followed, the procedure is identical. After sawing the planks to shape, they must be thoroughly glued together under pressure. A high-quality glue is essential, as is accuracy in line-up. Several cramps will be needed to provide an even pressure, and these can be made very simply, as detailed in Chap. II. Plate III shows a hull glued up under pressure.

While the glue is drying, a set of templates should be prepared by tracing off the body plan on to thin ply, stiff card, or even thin metal. The outside of the hull is then carved to approximate shape, using chisel, plane, spokeshave, rasp, etc., and making rough checks with the templates. When the final shape is emerging, accurate pencil lines should be drawn at the template stations to assist the work. Always use the cutting tools "downhill" on the grain, and never take off huge cuts. Finish this stage with coarse glasspaper, since small scars are likely to be sustained during hollowing the interior and these will be removed in the final glasspapering.

The interior is hollowed by using a brace and bit to drill closely-spaced holes where much material has to be removed. An odd length of tube slipped over the bit shank and taped to the chuck can be used as a depth gauge.

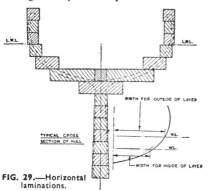

FIG. 29.—Horizontal laminations.

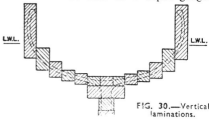

FIG. 30.—Vertical laminations.

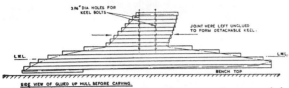

3/16" DIA HOLES FOR KEEL BOLTS

JOINT HERE LEFT UNGLUED TO FORM DETACHABLE KEEL.

L.W.L. — L.W.L.

BENCH TOP

SIDE VIEW OF GLUED UP HULL BEFORE CARVING.

FIG. 28.—Bread and buttering on the waterlines.

The remaining material is pared away with a gouge, again taking light cuts down the grain. It is well worth making a pair of double-ended calipers (Fig. 32) for checking wall thickness as work proceeds. The interior should be finished smooth with successive grades of glasspaper when the designer's specified hull weight is within reach.

Deck-beams and other reinforcements should be added (Fig. 35) and the exterior polished up with fine glasspaper before proceeding with the initial painting stages.

FIG. 31.—Use of templates.

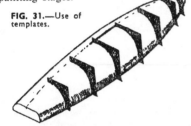

Rib and Plank

This system offers a rather lighter hull and is thus possibly more frequently found among model yachts than power boats. Material requirements are a little more stringent, since a finished hull can more easily twist or "starve" out of shape, but less heavy work is required to build a hull by this method. The following description applies to a yacht hull, but may equally be applied to other craft.

The first requirement is a jig, which

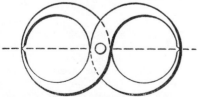

FIG. 32.—Double-ended calipers.

may be a flat plank of 1 in. x 4 in. or so, slightly longer than the hull to be built. Occasionally a second piece of timber is screwed beneath the first to form a "T", which ensures that the first board cannot assume a curve during building. Shadows, usually of ¼ in. ply, are now cut and fitted to the jig. Each shadow

FIG. 33.—Holding a hull for outside carving.

is traced off a body section on the body plan, but since these sections show the outside line of the finished hull, allowance must be made for the thickness of the planking and the ribs. Where the shadows will remain as bulkheads in the finished hull, only the planking thickness is allowed for, of course. The shadows are extended at the top so that the extended tops all fall on a straight line (Fig. 36), and they are secured upside down on the jig either by cutting notches in the jig and pinning them in, or by screwing a ½ in. square fillet to the top of each and screwing into each fillet from the underside of the jig (Fig. 37). Notches for keel and inwales must

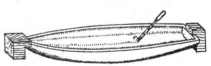

FIG. 34.—Holding a hull for inside carving.

be provided in the shadows, and they must be very accurately positioned on the jig.

The keel, stem, and sternpost assembly (the backbone) is next assembled directly over the plan; in the case of a yacht this is normally one smooth sweep of timber, and is best laminated from several strips of ⅛ in. material (Fig. 38), the width corresponding to the plank width at the midsection, i.e. ¾ in. for A hulls.

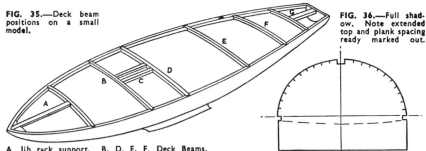

FIG. 35.—Deck beam positions on a small model.

FIG. 36.—Full shadow. Note extended top and plank spacing ready marked out.

A. Jib rack support. B, D, E, F. Deck Beams. C. Mast slide supports. G. Rudder trunk and/or vane support.

$\frac{5}{8}$ in. for 10 Raters and Marbleheads, and $\frac{1}{2}$ in. for 36R models, etc. When thoroughly dry, the backbone is dropped in place in the shadows, and the inwales similarly positioned and glued to the

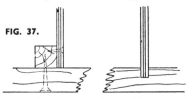

FIG. 37.

stem and transom, either direct, or by means of the breasthook, etc. Blocks, suitably rebated, are usually employed at the extreme bow and stern (Fig. 39).

Usually $\frac{1}{16}$ in. ply is used for the ribs. and this is cut into $\frac{1}{4}$ in. strips fitting round each shadow from the keel to the inwale. A little additional strength may be gained by jointing the ribs into the backbone and inwales, but the most important thing is to see that the ribs are flush with the other members. Tem-

porary pins can be tapped in to hold them to the curve of the shadows. Check alignment by laying a strip of planking in place.

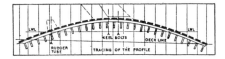

FIG. 38.—Backbones may be laminated in jigs made up of small wood blocks, or sawn from the solid.

The planks are normally cut from $\frac{1}{8}$ in. material—slightly thicker for the bigger classes. The planking must be set out on the body plan by stepping off the largest section to the required plank width (see above) and diagonalising as in Fig. 41. Note that most of

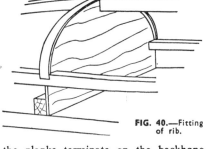

FIG. 40.—Fitting of rib.

the planks terminate on the backbone and do not run from end to end. The approximate plank width at each section can be taken off this "planking plan".

Mark out two sheer planks (one left and one right if your material is planed on one face only) leaving the top edge

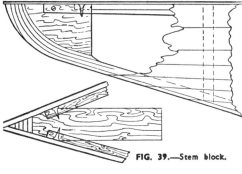

FIG. 39.—Stem block.

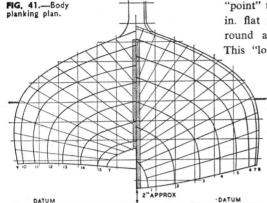

FIG. 41.—Body planking plan.

2" APPROX

DATUM   DATUM

"point" thus formed is planed off to $\frac{1}{4}$-$\frac{3}{8}$ in. flat and a strip of wood fastened round and planed to correct section. This "locks" the planks and moreover prevents them splitting if the boat has the misfortune to ride over a hard obstacle.

When planking is completed the hull must be planed off to receive the garboard piece (Fig. 45) and great care must be exercised to ensure a perfectly true surface. The garboard piece is cut from a single block, and is best fitted by drill-

straight; make sure that the marks made for the widths at the section stations join in a smooth curve. Cut and plane the curved edge, square to the face, and glue in place (planed face in if not planed both sides). Normally the deck will be screwed on top of the planking, but if you wish to let it in allowance must be made for this. The planks may be pinned in place (some experts use bootmaker's tingles for this),

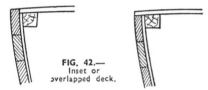

FIG. 42.— Inset or overlapped deck.

the pins being withdrawn when the glue is dry.

The second pair of planks is now prepared in exactly the same way, except that the top (straight) edges will require the faintest of bevels to fit snugly. Continue in this way. When the after ends of the planks approach the backbone, glue and pin a strip of planking over the backbone, about $\frac{1}{4}$ in. narrower, from the transom to the after end of the deadwood, to form a rebate to receive the plank ends. The forward plank ends are alternately overlapped (Fig. 44) over the backbone, and when all the planking is completed, the

STRIP SAME THICKNESS AS PLANKING

REBATE FORMED BY STRIP, FOR PLANKING

KEEL OR BACKBONE

PLANKING IN PROGRESS

FIG. 43.—Forming a rebate for the after planks.

ing the keel bolt holes through it and the backbone, and bolting together while the glue dries. The piece is then faired into the body and the planking can be cleaned up.

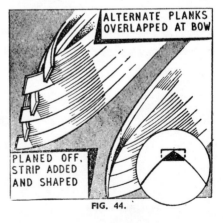

ALTERNATE PLANKS OVERLAPPED AT BOW

PLANED OFF, STRIP ADDED AND SHAPED

FIG. 44.

FIG. 45.—Planing off for the garboard piece.

Scrape off any surplus glue and withdraw all pins. Run a plane lightly over the "corners", and glasspaper with a coarse paper in all directions. Proceed with progressively finer grades of paper, lightly damping the hull to raise softer fibres, until a reasonable surface exists.

Before moving the hull mark out the slot for the skeg and drill and chisel right through the backbone. The skeg

itself is cut and fitted in the slot; for additional strength it may run right through to deck level (Fig. 47). Check that the alignment is perfect before gluing permanently in place.

Now remove the building jig, leaving the shadows in place, and bolt the hull to the bench or to a strip of timber held in a vice Knock or twist out the shadows, working from ends to middle, and clean up the inside of the hull shell. Any further internal reinforcement must now be added; this is usually limited to load-spreading members designed to dis-

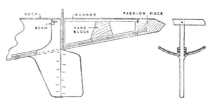

FIG. 47.—Skeg and other aft details.

tribute the stresses of the heavy lead keel (Fig. 48). A handle is usually incorporated for carrying the hull (Fig. 49). At this stage, too, the first coat or two of the interior varnish may be brushed on (see Chap. IX).

FIG. 48.—Athwartship load-spreader to take side strains of lead keel.

The next job is to fit the deck beams. These are cut to length and planed to correct camber (if a cambered deck is employed) from similar material to that used for the inwales. The beams are then halved into the inwales and fitted flush (Fig. 50). These beams are positioned to stiffen the deck and also to provide anchorages for various deck fittings. Fig. 35 shows a typical lay-out.

Ply is normally employed for the deck, and this is cut to shape and cleaned up,

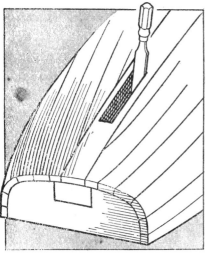

FIG. 46.—Chiselling the skeg slot.

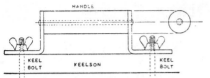

FIG. 49.—Internal carrying handle.

FIG. 50.—Deck beam/inwale jointing.

but not fitted until the interior is fully varnished, etc. The hatch, however, may be cut and the cover fitted ; this is located over the keel fixing bolts and the aperture should be large enough to admit a hand. The hatch cover is normally a rectangle of mahogany, etc., about ¼ in. larger all round than the hatch, to which is cemented a plug tightly fitting the hole ; this may also be of timber but a better job can be made by using sheet cork.

The remaining job is the fin keel, which is shaped from one block of wood. The entire fin is shaped and later cut to provide the pattern for the lead,

which, when cast and cleaned up, is bolted through the remaining portion of the fin (the deadwood) in the manner described in Chap. VIII.

Many types of hull can be built on the rib and plank system, following the general principles outlined above. Most will be simpler ; for example, a small trawler hull would use a block stem and counter with planking between, and would require no garboard piece or skeg, etc. Where sharp changes of curvature occur, planking can be difficult, so that the drawings for a proposed model should be carefully considered before deciding on rib and plank construction.

Chapter Five

Other Types of Construction

THERE are several other systems for building which apply to specific types of hull or to the working facilities available. Many of them are variants or combinations of methods already described, but one or two are completely different.

"Two-shelf" Chine Hulls

It will be obvious that a hard-chine hull is five-sided, the widest "side" being the deck. If we make the deck a primary structural member in the form of a complete shelf sawn to plan-shape, and make the chines in the same way, we have only to add a keelson or keel assembly to provide the "fifth corner" (Fig. 51). *Lorelei* and *Water Bug* (Plate III) are built on this system, which was first popularised by the author. Its chief advantages are the ease with which a symmetrical hull is produced, the positive fixing for the ply skins, and the small amount of internal structure necessary. Camber may be planed into the deck, and if pliant timber is used, deck sheer and chine curve can be incorporated by judiciously placed bulkheads and diagonal bracing (Fig. 52). Naturally, the system is not quite scale boat-building, and has its limitations, but for ease of building and overall strength it has much to commend it.

Composite Hulls

Quite a number of full-size ship types lend themselves to the simplified construction shown in Fig. 53, common examples being destroyers and oil tankers. The bow and the stern are the only parts deviating from a squarish cross-section, so these are built up on the bread and butter principle, with the midships portion employing only three planks for the bottom and sides. The thickness of these planks allows for the hull section to be carved in, but when thin planks are used a fillet can be fitted into the corner to preserve strength (Fig. 54).

Thick-bottom Hulls

In some cases of boats similar to the foregoing, it is possible to use one thick plank for the hull bottom and erect ply sides for most of the rest of the hull. The sides normally need to terminate on a bulkhead towards the stern, and the stern itself is then planked on a light frame or even bread-and-buttered. The round of the bilge will determine the thickness of the bottom plank (Fig. 54).

Diagonalled Bilge Hulls

The diagonal-planking system described in Chapter II, is excellent for round bilge hulls, with or without permanent bulkheads. The one difference in setting up for planking is that stringers are necessary in addition to ribs. These must be flush with the ribs and spaced about 2 in. apart, running from the extreme bow to the stern. The planks are laid on in exactly the same manner as for a chine hull, and joined to the backbone in the same way as

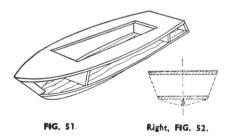

FIG. 51.   **Right, FIG. 52.**

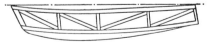

normal planks. The second layer can be laid on fore and aft instead of diagonally, if preferred, with no measurable effect on the ultimate strength. When applying diagonals, the width is governed by the amount of curvature, i.e., the planks will be narrower at the ends than the centre with an average hull. A trial strip will quickly determine whether the width is too great.

Gum-Strip Hulls

The enormous strength of laminated gum-strip paper is not generally realised. If you require to be convinced, soak a length of good quality gummed brown paper strip and wind it carefully round a broom-handle (over an ordinary sheet of paper so that it will slide off) until it approaches $\frac{1}{16}$ in. thick. Allow to dry thoroughly or bake the tube in a cool oven for an hour, and then try to collapse it. It can be done, of course, but the force required is quite astonishing.

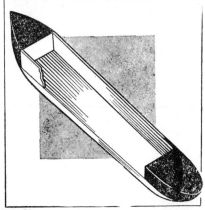

FIG. 53.

FIG. 54.—Corner fillets and thick hull bottoms.

Hulls can be built of this material quite easily and with very satisfactory results. A very light armature is necessary, and the best way is to cut ply bulkheads, notch them to receive $\frac{1}{16}$ sq. stringers, and set them up in a jig. The stringers need only be $\frac{1}{16}$ in. balsa, but they must be spaced no more than $\frac{1}{2}$ in. apart on sharp curves. A heavier inwale is desirable, since a ply deck will be screwed to this. Thoroughly soak the strip and lay it on round the hull first, then diagonally each way, then fore and aft. Repeat until a good thickness is built up—$\frac{1}{16}$ in. is adequate for most purposes. Only short lengths need be used, and care should be taken to avoid too many air bubbles. When completely dry, rub the outside down and apply one or two coats of shellac. Rub down again, and shellac five or six times more, rubbing down between each coat. The inside also requires several coats of

shellac. Varnishing or painting thus has a hard base and is carried out normally. A hull built in this way is a fraction heavier than a wood-planked hull, but a first-class job in every respect.

Papier Mache Hulls

This method is rather a misnomer, since the paper used is not pulped completely. Frankly, it is an evil-smelling process offering little advantage over the previous system except that it is very cheap. Tear a large quantity of old newspapers into squares of 3 in. or 4 in., and drop them in a bucket of water into which has been dissolved a packet of glue size. They should soak for a

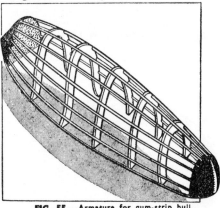

FIG. 55.—Armature for gum-strip hull.

day or so before being used. An armature similar to that described above is needed, but the stringers may be spaced further apart. Lay the squares of paper in place on the frame until three or four layers have been built up, then allow to dry off slightly. Brush thin glue over ("toffee" glue will do) and add a couple of layers, brush on more glue, add layers, etc., until a thickness of $\frac{1}{8}$ in. or so has been reached. Finish exactly as above.

Strawboard Hulls

Strawboard is a low-grade type of card, usually grey or fawn in colour, used for packing, etc. Hulls can be built from this material, using it in exactly the same way as timber, and finishing with the shellac process described for the two previous methods. It is particularly suited to diagonal planking and offers the advantages of exceptionally low cost and easy availability of the material. Hulls built of strawboard demand patient workmanship to achieve first-class results, but are extremely strong and seaworthy when finished. Working is simplified by the flexibility of the material when damped.

Clincher Built Hulls

Clincher, or clinker, building, is a system of producing a hull with no internal framework, and incorporates overlapping planks (Fig. 56). Most ordinary rowing boats, dinghies, lifeboats, etc., are built in this way. Procedure is much the same as for normal planked hulls, except that sufficient width must be allowed in each plank for the overlap, and planking must start at the garboard, i.e., next to the keel. In full-size practice the planks are often merely pinned

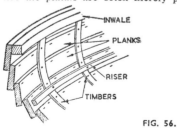

FIG. 56.

together, but in models it is usual to glue the overlap as well as pinning it. Ply is usually used for planks, since the pins are close to the edge and splitting is frequent with plain timber.

At the bow and stern, the top of each plank is chiselled off to a feather-edge for an inch or two ; this allows the next plank to seat down to a nice smooth finish. The pins, projecting inside, are snipped off after completing the planking, and clinched over inside. Timbers are now added (Fig. 56) by pinning through from outside and clinching over. Longitudinal stringers (risers) are added to support thwarts, etc.

Few boats greater than 30 ft. or so are built on this system, except for large ships' lifeboats and whalers, which may be as much as 70 ft. in length.

Fabric Hulls

Occasionally a very lightweight hull may be required, for example for rubber-powered speed models. This type of hull can be made by building a hard chine frame of as light construction as will do the job, and covering it with silk or nylon The material should be applied by soaking in water, blotting lightly in an old towel, and stretching on the frame using pins and a cellulose cement or thick clear dope. The adhesive will "blush" on contact with the wet fabric, but this will disappear when the material is treated with two or three coats of clear dope and a coat or two of banana oil. Alternatively, two or three coats of varnish may be applied.

Metal Hulls

The production of a metal hull is not difficult provided that the design takes into account the limitations of the material. To arrive at a design and to produce a set of templates, a hull should first be mocked-up in stiff card. Anyone capable of assembling a multi-piece metal hull will be experienced enough to know the limitations of his medium (Fig. 57 shows a typical boat for this type of construction). The beginner is advised to try the two-piece type of hull laid out in Fig. 58. The main section forms the hull itself, and

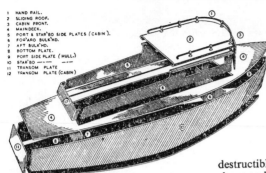

1 HAND RAIL.
2 SLIDING ROOF.
3 CABIN FRONT.
4 MAIN DECK.
5 PORT & STAR'BD SIDE PLATES (CABIN).
6 FOR'ARD BULK'HD.
7 AFT BULK'HD.
8 BOTTOM PLATE.
9 PORT SIDE PLATE (HULL.)
10 STAR'BD ———
11 TRANSOM PLATE
12 TRANSOM PLATE (CABIN)

FIG. 57.—An "exploded" sketch of a simple all-metal model.

the application of the resin-bonded glass fibre technique. Glass fibre, so treated, is outstanding in many ways, particularly in regard to strength/weight ratio. A hull of this material is virtually indestructible, and remains constant in shape and weight since it is impervious to heat as well as water, oil, and most other substances. There are two primary methods of using it for a hull: (a) armouring; and (b) moulding.

Armouring is fairly self-explanatory, and consists of encasing a hull in the glass and resin which, incidentally, will adhere to almost anything. The model is built in the normal way, except that it is planked in balsa (or carved from balsa) which is considerably easier and faster to work with; furthermore, the surface does not need to be perfect, i.e., planks need not meet exactly provided that the gaps do not exceed about ⅛ in. Now, glass fibre is available made up into broadly three different forms, glass tape, which is finely woven and has little application for our purposes, glass cloth, and chopped strand mat. Glass cloth

is cut from zinc or lead-coated steel of appropriate gauge. One or two wooden formers help to achieve the desired "rolled" shape and these may be permanently installed with screws or later replaced with metal frames. The second piece is the transom, and the assembly is tacked together with solder and cramps and trued up before the final joints are made. These are soldered with the aid of a blowlamp, soft iron wire ($\frac{3}{32}$ in. or 12 s.w.g.) being laid inside the corners to help form a fillet. Keel, etc., may be soldered in place, but the deck, motor mounting, etc., are best fitted by means of wood blocks secured to the hull by bolts or screws.

Glass Fibre Hulls

One of the most interesting post-war developments in the model boat world is

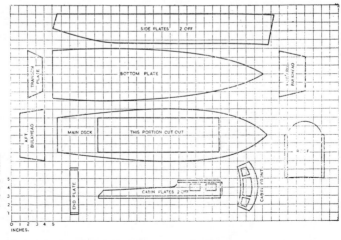

FIG. 57a. — The simple metal boat above laid out for scaling up. Structure is also suitable for an all-ply model if preferred.

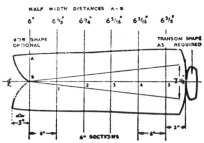

FIG. 58.—A 36 in. round bilge all-metal hull.

uses longer fibres than mat, and the latter is of looser weave. Cloth is the usual material, and it is laid over the model and the resin brushed on. The resin (a polyester type) requires the addition of a catalyst to cause it to cure, and this is mixed in before application.

A fairly stiff brush should be used to brush the resin on ; flow a coat over the model, press the cloth in position, and apply a second coat of resin, stippling well to remove air bubbles, which are the enemy of a successful job. The cloth is cut into workable pieces, allowing an overlap above the gunwale, and after the hull is completely covered a second layer may be brushed on over the first, taking care to leave a reasonable surface if possible. The time required for the resin to cure will depend on the amount of hardener added and the temperature in which the operation is carried out ; take a tip—if it starts to "go off" in the jar, throw it away. If you brush it on it will be lumpy and you will have hours of work filing the lumps down !

The brush and the hands can be cleaned by thorough washing in a detergent ; the hull will require to be left until it is really hard to the touch. Incidentally, it is rather smelly until completely hard. The surface must now be rubbed down with coarse grit paper, progressing to finer grades and filling and painting in the normal way.

A moulded hull can be made using either a male or a female mould, the latter being more trouble but preferable

since a much superior surface is obtained on the face actually contacting the mould. The easiest material for the mould is plaster of paris, although a carved wooden one is quite suitable.

To make a male plaster mould, a set of normal body section templates and a template of the complete profile of the hull are required, allowing for the thickness of the glass fibre and raising the deck-line about 1 in. Nail odd blocks of wood to a board to fill most of the space to be occupied by the mould, to reduce the amount of plaster required. Take about a quart of water in a suitable container, and scatter plaster in while stirring, till a consistency approaching that of thick cream is reached, then rapidly apply to the mould. Repeat, building up a hull form rather larger than will be required ; wet plaster will not adhere well to plaster already set, so score the set plaster heavily to form a key. The finished shape will be ready for work within a few minutes —it is easier to scrape away fresh-set plaster than to wait until it has dried out thoroughly. Scrape the surface down until the templates almost fit, then leave for a day or so before glass-papering down to the final mould Thoroughly shellac the surface with half-a-dozen coats.

A female mould may be built in the same way, or may be taken off a male (either specially made or a hull of which a copy is desired), if no undercuts exist, by greasing the male all over with a 50-50 mixture of Russian tallow and motor oil applied warm, and including in the greasing the board round the base of the male. Apply plaster over the grease, reinforcing with scraps of old cloth (muslin or similar open-weave material), bits of string, lengths of wood, etc., and building up a thickness of about 1 in. Plaster in two lengths of timber, held in with stout cloth straps, so that they will

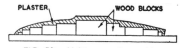

FIG. 59.—Making a male mould.

form a base when the female mould is inverted. Leave a day or so, then trim any odd lumps which may bond the mould to the baseboard, and remove, using the two battens as grips and also prising round the base. Invert the mould and leave to dry out a little more before lightly sanding the interior and shellacking as above.

The more usual way of making a female mould is to use a plaster or wood pattern and treat it thoroughly with parting agent, then paint on resin and apply glass cloth in the manner described below. This produces a glass-fibre mould, usually of a good enough finish to mould a hull from straight away. Where there are undercuts, etc., a two-piece mould is made by building a $\frac{1}{2}$ in. high Plasticine wall along the centre line, applying parting agent to this and half the hull, and moulding a flange in the half-hull, against the Plasticine. When cured, the wall is scraped away, the flange and other half painted with parting agent, and the other half-hull moulded, also with a flange. The flanges are then drilled through for bolts before removal from the pattern, then the halves are bolted together ready to mould the finished hull; they have to be unbolted to remove the hull, after it has cured.

Before commencing the actual hull, the mould must be treated with a parting agent; stearic acid is best, but floor or furniture polish can be used. One coat of resin may now be brushed on and left to dry, following which a layer of cloth may be positioned and resin brushed over it. Normally three thicknesses of cloth are used, with extra strips laid round points of stress such as the stem. Internal timber members can be laid in place on wet resin and reinforced with glass cloth, and, for a yacht, the garboard piece can be laid in place in the

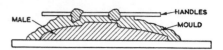

FIG. 60.—Making a female plaster mould from a male or from an existing hull.

same way, filleted (or faired) in with unravelled strands of cloth pushed in and thoroughly coated with resin.

Two advantages of the resin are that it will always bond to itself, i.e., wet resin applied to dry will set as an integral member, and, at the sacrifice of a little drying time, it can be coloured with litho ink so that the colour is constant throughout. The former is useful for adding inwales, etc., and effecting repairs, and the latter allows a "plastic" finish without painting; scratches can be simply polished out. The material can also be sawn, filed, drilled, etc., and metal parts can be bonded in place as the same way as wood.

When the hull shell is thoroughly dry (with normal amounts of hardener, 1½ hours at 70° F. to be work-dry, but a little longer to cure completely) saw off the ragged edge above the gunwale and remove from the mould. The surface can now be smoothed down with emery or glasspaper, followed by fine carborundum paper. The internal details can be fixed with wet resin, etc., and a brushload can be applied to any flaws in the exterior to build up sufficient surplus matter to be cut down again to the true surface. Polishing of coloured resin is carried out with 400 wet-or-dry paper followed by an abrasive metal polish such as "Brasso", and two or three coats of Simoniz car polish. The procedure for painting uncoloured resin is the same as that for wood hulls, except that since the resin is completely waterproof, fewer coats are needed.

Chapter Six

Superstructures

FOR the purposes of this chapter, a superstructure is any part of the boat from the deck up which requires constructional work. Fittings are dealt with in the next chapter.

A word or two on decks may not be amiss here. The best deck is undoubtedly cut from ply and fitted in one piece or such pieces as may be required where the foredeck and/or afterdeck occupy different levels. Ply decks can be convincingly marked (Chap. IX), and it is not usually necessary to plank a deck unless the builder desires to do so, or unless a combination of extreme sheer and camber means that ply cannot be induced to take the curves.

FIG. 61.

The classic method of planking a deck is to fit a kingplank (often in a timber of contrasting colour) down the centre of the hull, its width being roughly ½ in. for a 3 ft. hull, and its thickness the same as that of the planking to be used. The two outside planks of the deck may be of the same colour wood, about ¼ in. wide, and a small sheet of the same timber can be fitted at the extreme bow and stern (Fig. 61), to provide a pleasing pattern. The planks themselves should be ⅜ in. wide to fit in with the above example, and they are laid parallel with the outer hull line from the outside inwards. As each plank is cut, the end

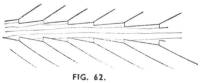

FIG. 62.

is shaped and laid over the king-plank, which is pared away to receive the plank ends (Fig. 62). This is known as "joggling in". When sanded smooth and varnished, a very attractive deck results.

A scale deck for a trawler, etc., will have the planks running straight fore and aft, but still requires the outer two planks to follow the shape of the hull (Fig. 63) to form the waterway. Where the deck is broken for a hatch, the planks terminate in a rebate on a plank laid thwartships, as in Fig. 64.

The built-up superstructure will normally be in the form of a cabin for a small boat, or a bridge and deckhouses, etc., for larger craft. The golden rule is to keep all this "top hamper" light in weight, and for maximum strength it is customary to make it in thin ply. Corners become rather difficult with thin materials, so corner-pieces of square

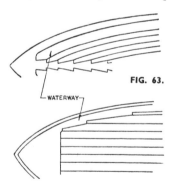

FIG. 63.

WATERWAY

timber are employed for reinforcement. Where a rounded corner exists, this is shaped from a piece of timber of sufficient section to give the required radius, and the sides, etc., are rebated in (Fig. 65).

Many deck-houses and so forth have cambered roofs, and these are usually set up on ply frames cut to give the required camber. The frames are fretted

p left is a bread-and-butter hull in
ps, below it, an attractive little four-
ed barque under full sail. Top right
.orelei", a simple example of two shelf
.ruction. Centre left is an all-metal
el employing the hull shown in Chapter
entre right a magnificent Swiss scale ship
el. Lower left shows a powerful electric
r driving four propellor shafts through

an open frame gear box; note flexible
rubber tube connections. Above is
"Waterbug", a small all-balsa model
again employing two shelf construction, while on the left is an example
of near-scale modelling, the electric
paddle steamer "Royal Falcon",
again of balsa construction.

PLATE 3.

Left are two views of a small yacht, actually the "Water Baby" design show[n] Plate 7. This hull is built on the v[e] bread-and-butter system, and the dif[ference in] grain in the planks can be seen in the pic[ture]

Large and heavy boats such as those fitting the A class rule are frequently built on the bread-and-butter system as in this example of laminating on the buttocks. The photograph shows the hull and fin glued up ready for carving to commence.

The picture on the left, taken in [the] "Model Maker" workshop, shows a Ma[rble-]head hull ready for planking. Strips of [wood] have been inserted beneath the ribs to e[nsure] easy removal of the shadows at a later s[tage]

Here the frame above has been completely planked and is ready to be cleaned up and smoothed generally. Note the T-section building jig and the square fillets by means of which the shadows are held to the jig, also the flat garboard piece seating.

The completed hull with fin and ske[g in] position and requiring only the additio[n of] fore-and-aft deck members. The ribs [can] clearly be seen, as can the backbone; [the] absence of other internal structural mem[bers] is worth noticing.

PLATE 4.

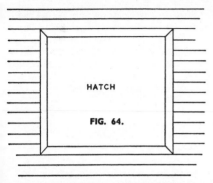

HATCH

FIG. 64.

the interior, and it must therefore be strong enough to withstand a certain amount of handling. The joint around the base should be watertight, since few models avoid splashes on the deck during operation, and a fast boat in particular produces spray which, while it may be thrown clear in calm weather, is often blown over the boat in a breeze. To prevent water seeping in, a flange can be fitted to the deck all round each hatch, over which the superstructure fits (Fig. 68). Additional protection can be given to a non-scale boat by fitting a soft, thin-walled rubber tube outside this flange, the superstructure being

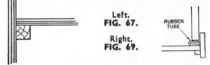

Left,
FIG. 67.

RUBBER TUBE

Right,
FIG. 69.

clipped down in such a way as to squash the tube and provide an excellent seal.

out to save weight, and must be positioned between any ports or windows. Fig. 66 shows a typical cabin structure made in this way. Curved fronts, etc., require horizontal formers, and should be cut so that the natural bend of the ply helps assembly. All ply-to-ply joints should be made with the aid of a fillet strip which need be no more than ⅛ in. square (Fig. 67).

The plain flange round the aperture will usually prove sufficient to retain the superstructure in place; alternatively, dowels can be mounted in small blocks glued in each corner of the unit, plugging into corresponding holes in blocks glued in the hatch. When a positive, quick-action clip is desired, mount Terry clips at each end (or in each corner) of the superstructure and provide spigots to engage them in the hull itself (Fig. 70). Springs or rubber bands are sometimes

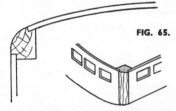

FIG. 65.

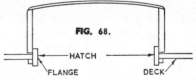

FIG. 68.

HATCH

FLANGE   DECK

Metal such as thin aluminium or tinplate can be used for superstructures, using riveted or soldered joints, but little advantage is gained, and unless a considerable saving in weight can be effected there is little point in using such materials.

Frequently, the cabin or other superstructure is removable to allow access to

used (Fig. 71), but take longer to hook up.

Hatches may also be fitted and sealed in the above ways, except where a flush hatch is needed. This often arises when the superstructure is too small to provide adequate access, and it is therefore secured to the deck and a portion of the deck made to lift out. Fig. 72 shows a suitable seal for this type of joint.

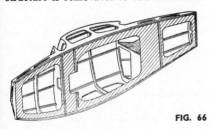

FIG. 66

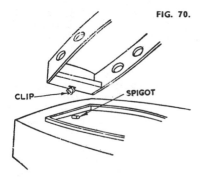

FIG. 70.

CLIP   SPIGOT

As an alternative to removable cabins, etc., some boats have only the top removable. This means that the structure offers no sealing difficulty around its base, and the chance of water entering is lessened by the extra inch or two of height, and also the fact that most tops will overhang the sides, front, etc., i.e., there is no corner to collect the water. A simple plug-in top is therefore satisfactory (Fig. 73).

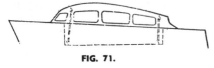

FIG. 71.

When a considerable amount of equipment is carried, or access is otherwise required on a large scale (as with some steam plants) most of the deck is made detachable. In this case the inwales are better if slightly more generous, and a strip of rubber (aircraft type, or cut from a cycle inner tube) can be cemented in place to form a water seal. Quick release fittings can be made by soldering tags on small screws, the tags passing through slots in the inwales and tightening the deck down by running over a sprung ramp fitted to the inwale (Fig. 74). Such decks are usually inset below the hull planking, of course (Fig. 42), and should have a normal hatch for access to the motor.

FIG. 72.

Most superstructures are fitted with ports or windows, ports being used where there is a chance of volumes of water breaking over. Ports are as a rule flush with the external surface, i.e.,

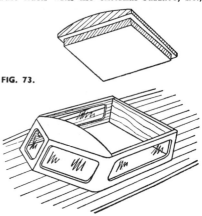

FIG. 73.

they do not have a projecting rim, although with small boats a brass flange may be visible. The best representation is simply a cleanly cut hole with celluloid behind it, but this is unsatisfactory if the material thickness is greater than about $\frac{1}{16}$ in. With thick material, it is best to drill the hole slightly oversize and cement in a seamless curtain ring

FIG. 74.

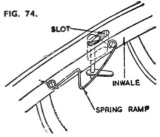

SLOT

INWALE

SPRING RAMP

flush with the surface (Durofix is excellent for this purpose). This forms a rebate against which a disc of celluloid may be cemented.

Windows, on the other hand, usually have a slightly raised frame or a bead on their outer faces, and are unlikely to be cut in anything thicker than $\frac{3}{8}$ in. ply. To produce the raised frame, cut

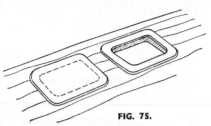

FIG. 75.

a blank from bristol board, veneer, or $\frac{1}{32}$ in. ply, to the outside shape, and cement accurately in place. Mark out the actual window and fret out. Alternatively, bend a bead from florists' or similar wire, and cement in place, or varnish a length of thread or fishing line, allow to dry drawn taut, and form the bead from the resulting stiffened thread, cemented in place. The celluloid is cemented behind the window.

For such purposes, celluloid or clear acetate sheeting can be used. It pays to use these materials in a thickness of at least .010 in., and the shapes can be

cut by merely scratching the surface and cracking the shape out. Coins and washers of various sizes help to cut true circles, but if you are building a liner model it is well worth investing in a punch for cutting accurate port glasses. The celluloid or acetate should be cemented in place *before* painting, using Durofix ; scraps of paper can be stuck

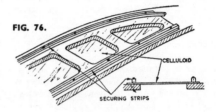

FIG. 76.

in place with soap to mask the glazing off during painting. A line of cabin windows can be glazed after painting if required, by using one long strip of celluloid held in place by $\frac{1}{16}$ in. x $\frac{1}{8}$ in. strips pinned along its edges.

Chapter Seven   **Fittings**

THE question of fittings for the average semi-scale launch type of model is one that is entirely up to the individual builder. Near-scale models must have a certain minimum of detail, and this can be patterned after that used for scale boats. Yacht fittings are in a separate class, of course, and are dealt with in another chapter. Certain items are found under different guises in various forms of models, and it will therefore be advisable if we work through the various fittings from the simplest to the advanced. As with the superstructure, light weight for all fittings is essential.

FIG. 77.   FIG. 78.

Launch types usually have a mooring post and a pair of towing posts, fair-leads to suit, handrails, a ventilator or two, usually of the airscoop type, and possibly steaming and riding lights and a syren. The posts are easily made from pieces of square timber with a drilled hole in which is driven a stub of brass wire (Fig. 78). All edges are bevelled, and cuts are taken out of the four corners below the wire to produce a waisted effect. In full scale, the posts run down to main hull members, so if they are mounted in the corners of a well, their full length must be shown.

Fairleads are merely guides to contain a rope, and on small craft look like the top left example in Fig. 79. They can be carved from a

FIG. 79.

close-grained wood such as box, or cut from plastic or metal sheet.

Handrails on small boats are frequently cut from a length of timber as in Fig. 80, and are fitted directly to cabin tops, etc. Alternatively, they may be made by screwing in 000 brass screweyes, sliding through a length of brass wire, and soldering. Welding or brazing rod is the best brass wire, since it is hard-drawn (stiff) and usually dead straight. A further variation is to use split pins as the stanchions, epecially where a screw-eye offers insufficient length (Fig. 81).

Airscoop vents are difficult to fabricate, although not all that hard to carve from timber. A fairly easy system is to mould them from thick acetate sheet, carving a male mould and a matching hole in a small piece of ply. Soften the acetate by laying it over the mould in a warm oven (about 230° F. is average softening point), then push the piece of

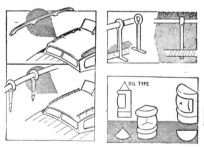

FIG. 80.   FIG. 81 (top) FIG. 82

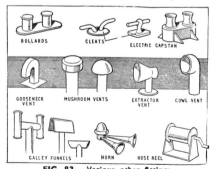

BOLLARDS   CLEATS   ELECTRIC CAPSTAN

GOOSENECK VENT   MUSHROOM VENTS   EXTRACTOR VENT   COWL VENT

GALLEY FUNNELS   HORN   HOSE REEL

FIG. 83.—Various other fittings.

ply over until fully home. Remove the moulding, cut the vent opening, and trim the base to shape.

Steaming and riding lights are usually quarter-round and half-round (Fig. 82), and may be carved from dowel or fabricated from scraps of wood or plastic. Coloured plastic beads (sold for children) can be cut to provide the lenses.

Syrens may be single or paired, and for small craft resemble modern motorcar external horns. The mechanism end offers little problem, but the bell is delicate and is best shaped from something like a plastic golf tee. The modeller making his own details soon acquires a stock of old toothbrush handles, wireless parts, and suchlike odds and ends, which, when raked over, frequently offer the solution to minor problems !

Larger boats than those so far begin to sport such things as bollards, cleats, cowl vents, chain, rails, skylights, steer-

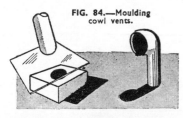

FIG. 84.—Moulding cowl vents.

ing wheels, etc. Bollards can be produced in wood, using dowel and thin ply discs on a ply base, or in metal, when the easiest way is to use brass screws or rivets, filed off flat on top and cut off to length, soldered to a brass base-plate. Cleats are metal versions of mooring posts on a smaller scale, and are simply made from split pins with soldered brass wires.

Cowl vents are another ticklish proposition—they never look satisfactory carved from wood, and small hollow balls which can be halved and cemented to dowels are not easily come by. The ends of some small pill containers, etc., can be cut off and used, but the easiest way is to mould the cowls from acetate sheet. A hemispheric mould (the end of a small test tube, for example), and

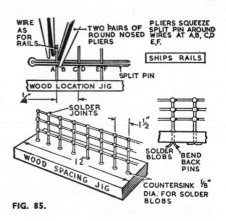

FIG. 85.

a suitable hole drilled in a piece of ply are the simplest requirements ; the acetate is cut into squares, softened (230° F.), and each cowl is individually formed by pushing through the hole with the mould. For mass production, lay various-sized ball bearings on a metal tray and pop in a low oven. Lay the acetate over the bearings and warm, when it will drop over the balls. This can be aided by light pressure with a soft foam rubber sponge. Carefully trim the resulting hemispheres and cement them to appropriate diameter dowels trimmed to a suitable angle and length.

Chain is best purchased, but if you wish to make it, it can be done by winding phosphor-bronze or brass wire tightly on another wire of a diameter corresponding to the link size required. A long cut is then made with a fine saw

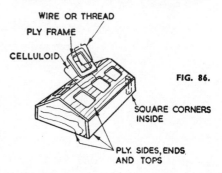

FIG. 86.

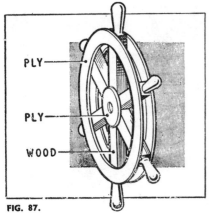

PLY

PLY

WOOD

FIG. 87.

can be brass wire and the lower ones stranded cable (wire ropes are customary on smallish vessels). The only suitable cable is "Laystrate" wire sold for control-line model aircraft, and not too much paint must be used or the effect of the stranded wire will be lost.

Skylights are relatively simple if built up from thin ply as in Fig. 86. If it is desired to hinge the frames, this is best done by means of a strip of silk glued in place. Frosted glass may be simulated by rubbing the acetate with fine glasspaper, two good strokes at 90° being best. The safety bars stand proud of the frames and should be made from copper wire, the ends being pinched to flatten them.

Another difficult detail is the steering wheel. In fairly large scale (1½ in. dia-

or knife-edge file along one side of the coil, so that the turns are all severed, and may be slid off as cut links. They are then fitted together and each one is soldered (place solder paste on each and pass through a flame), after which a narrow wire is slipped into each in turn and the links squeezed to ovality with pliers.

Rails are a problem in that stanchions need to be turned for perfect results. However, long fine split pins can be modified with patience (Fig. 85), or the rail can be laid out on a block, the longitudinals passed through the plain split pins, and the gaps in the sides of the pins filled with solder. The top rail

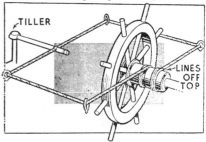

TILLER

LINES OFF TOP

FIG. 89.

meter or so) it is quite possible to make a wheel from thin ply discs and rings, with square spokes shaped only outside the outer ring (Fig. 87). Smaller wheels are easier in metal, and are best produced by drilling a tube for spokes and slicing off the drilled portion. The wire spokes are slipped through and soldered to a central washer, a second washer being soldered on the other side (Fig. 88). A few minutes with a needle file will shape the wire ends.

A working wheel can be constructed by adding a double pulley (made from washers) to the shaft, and winding on three or four turns of twine from each direction. The twine is led out athwartship, turned through smooth wire loops and taken aft, turned again and made off on the tiller. Spinning the wheel

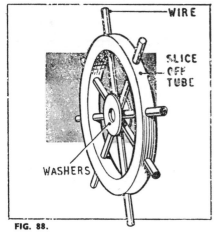

WIRE

SLICE OFF TUBE

WASHERS

FIG. 88.

either way will produce the correct rudder action only if the lines come off the *top* of the pulley (Fig. 89).

Lifebelts can be made from several things, fat curtain rings (especially bone and wood), being excellent. Alternatives are small rubber tyres, fishing rod rings, and similar items. Lifebelts normally have a line round them, secured to the belt by four equal-spaced whippings (Fig. 90) of about eight turns. It is quite sufficient to cement the ends of the whippings, which makes a neat job ; the method of producing blind ends is shown in Fig. 91, and may be used if preferred. A little trouble in finding a thread or twine with a pronounced twist is well worthwhile—it looks so much more like scale rope.

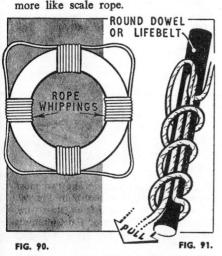

FIG. 90.   FIG. 91.

Masts are made from timber as a rule, with birch dowel being first choice. Tapering is a rather tedious business, but may be hastened by planing the dowel on four sides before applying glasspaper. Mast caps (Fig. 92) can be cut from thin ply or thick celluloid. Metal tube can be used for masts, particularly the cheaply available war surplus tapered aerials, but light weight is still an essential requirement. Step masts in blocks screwed to bulkheads, or pass them through the deck right down to a step screwed to the keelson. If a mast

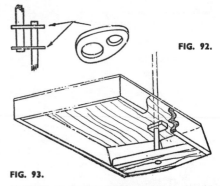

FIG. 92.

FIG. 93.

is fitted to a detachable unit, it should extend through to the bottom of the unit (Fig. 93) for really rigid anchorage.

Rigging is always rather a nuisance, since nine times out of ten it will interfere with the removal of part of the superstructure. One way round is to use shirring elastic where possible, providing a small hook to engage an eye at the foot of the stay or shroud. Where three or four shrouds make off close together, they can be made off to a wire engaging in clips on the bulwark, etc. Another way is to terminate each line in a tiny coil spring which, while only comprising three or four turns, is enough to tension the rigging. Permanent rigging can be made from "Laystrate" wire.

Most boats employ at least a few rigging blocks, the most frequent types being stropped blocks and sheaved blocks. Stropped blocks can be made from dowel with the aid of needle files (Fig. 94), and are more or less permanent fixtures. Sheaved blocks include a pulley, and may be single, double, or treble. The pulley can be filed from dowel and drilled before parting off, and fitted with a strap or case made from

FIG. 94.

FIG. 95.

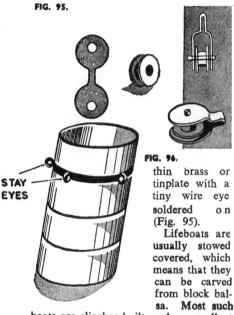

STAY
EYES

FIG. 96.

obviating the need to hollow the hull. Cheap toy plastic boats are frequently suitable for dinghies, etc., after slight modifications, but if you wish to make your own boats completely, they can be made in the same way as larger models, or carved from the solid (lime or obeche give good results) with the aid of lino-cutting gouges.

Rolled gummed paper is perfectly satisfactory for funnels, though for a more scale-like thickness brass shim with a soldered seam is preferable. Tinplate is often used, and the funnel bands are also of brass or tinplate cut into narrow strips, or wire soldered into place. Steam pipes and syrens can be fabricated quite simply from thin-walled brass tube, or, if bends are required, copper tube.

thin brass or tinplate with a tiny wire eye soldered on (Fig. 95).

Lifeboats are usually stowed covered, which means that they can be carved from block balsa. Most such

boats are clincher built, and an excellent representation can be obtained by carving the hull slightly undersize and glueing on paper planks—rather a fiddley business, but producing an excellent result. The canvas covers should be added after, from bristol board or ply, since it is not easy to carve the tops flat enough to be convincing. Boats stowed without covers are usually secured inverted, again

Anchors can be made up from the scrap box, copper being extremely use-

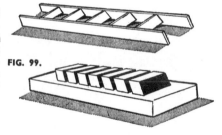

FIG. 99.

ful since it works easily. The two most common patterns are shown in Fig. 97.

Davits can be formed from brass wire, suitably tapered, or, if of the Columbus pattern (Fig. 98), cut from ply and brought to the required width with wood fairings. A drilled hole or a stub of brass tube held in place with a silk patch will provide a pivot if the davits are to be fully working.

A small jig should be constructed for the assembly of ladders (Fig. 99). Metal ladders are a straightforward soldering job in wire, and wood-type ones can be made in ply or in soldered brass shim.

The building of winches, capstans, and so on is greatly aided by an assortment of old clock parts, cotton reels, electrical coil bobbins, and the like. In these, as with other detail, photographs

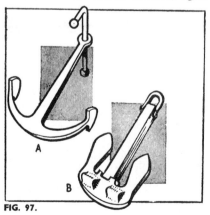

A

B

FIG. 97.

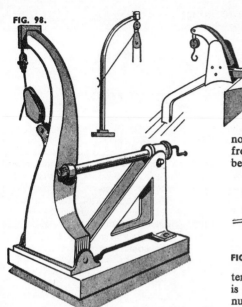

FIG. 98.

Above, small boat and liner davits; left, Columbus pattern davit.

foot of hull length is a rough guide. It is customary nowadays to balance the rudder (Fig. 102) to reduce the force required to turn it, except on full-keel or scale models (Fig. 103), although even this type of rudder can be partially balanced, as shown in the sketch.

A friction adjustment is necessary if no radio is fitted and the boat will be free-running, and this can be cut and bent up from brass (Fig. 104). An al-

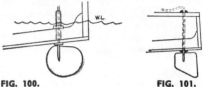

FIG. 100.   FIG. 101.

ternative, where the tiller is not required, is to thread the rudder stock to receive nuts and a washer (or solder a washer in place) compressing a short coil spring

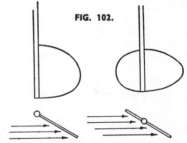

FIG. 102.

which in effect jams the rudder at the bottom. The adjusting knob can frequently be disguised as an item of ship's gear.

A complete book could be written in describing various detail fittings, but

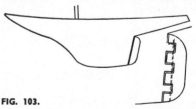

FIG. 103.

of full-size gear are of considerable assistance in obtaining an authentic appearance.

The rudder is an important part of any model, and is usually cut from brass sheet and soldered in a saw-cut in a length of brass rod. The rod passes through a bush in the hull (Fig. 100), or through a tube located by soldered washers (Fig. 101). It is important that the top of the bush or tube is well above the waterline to prevent leaks. Thick paint should be flowed into the bottom assembly with a screwed bush, for the same purpose; with soldered washers, the bottom should be soldered first, then paint flowed round and the top washer slipped in place. Rivet the end of the tube over, to draw the bottom up tight, before soldering.

Rudder shape is only important in high speed radio models; beginners and simple models need only worry about movement (25 deg. each side) and area, though it is hard to give a general rule for area. About 1¼ sq. in. per

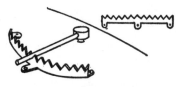

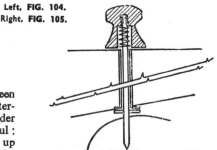

Left, **FIG. 104.**
Right, **FIG. 105.**

most of the common ones have been
touched on above. In addition to materials so far mentioned, the scale builder
will find paxolin tube extremely useful :
it is available in sizes of from ⅛ in. up
to 2½ in. diameter, is light in weight,
and can be cemented. For torpedo tubes,
circular hatches, small gun turrets and
barbettes, and all other parts calling for
largish tubing, it is invaluable. Paxolin
or fibre sheet is also handy for many
jobs.

Naturally, most ship fittings can be
purchased ready-made and give a very
professional-looking air to a model.
Many modellers, however, derive great
satisfaction from using their ingenuity to
reproduce detail, and it is surprising what
everyday things can be pressed into service. Cut-off radio valves or ground-off
wine glasses make excellent turrets for
air/sea rescue launches, old torch reflec-
tors are excellent for certain types of
radar scanner, sections of combs provide
fiddley gratings, and so on. Finally, if
you think something improves your
model, add it—it's *your* model. Some
people are horrified at shoe eyelets being
used for port rims, but on certain types
of simple model they add to the model's
appearance, so use them !

Chapter Eight   **Yacht Fittings**

THE fittings required for a model yacht differ from those in the previous chapter in that they are strictly functional. Generally speaking, much the same fittings are required whatever the yacht, although naturally the bigger the model the stronger the fittings must be.

In constructing the hull we made the complete fin up in wood. This must now be cut to provide the pattern for casting the lead, and the cut piece must be thoroughly painted or shellacked, and smoothed to a good finish. Now make two rough boxes a little larger than the pattern, open on one face, and matching fairly well when the open faces are together. Drill the top of the pattern and insert two dowels spaced so that they exactly fit the keel bolt holes, and cut the boxes to allow the dowels to protrude through one side. Grease the pattern and dowels. Now mix sufficient plaster of paris to fill one of the boxes, making it slightly on the runny side. Fill the box and place the pattern on to the wet plaster, pushing down until it is exactly half submerged. Check that the dowels are in position, and hold for a few seconds until the plaster has set.

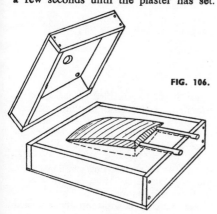

FIG. 106.

Drill small holes in three corners of the back of the second box, and a larger hole in the other corner. Shellac the face of the set plaster and grease lightly, then place the second box in position and pour in plaster until overflowing. Allow to set, then gently separate the boxes and remove the pattern. Chase out the plaster to make a filling hole (Fig. 107), and at the highest point of the mould a breather hole. Bake the two moulds or allow to dry out thoroughly for a few days.

FIG. 107.

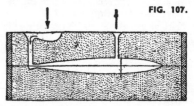

Bend two lengths of studding to form "hockey-sticks", and lay them in place in the holes formed by the dowels. Slip nuts on to prevent them sliding too far in, and check that adequate thread projects for passing up into the boat. Now strap the boxes together firmly and stand between a couple of bricks, or similar. Cut into small pieces slightly more lead than will be needed for the finished casting, and melt down in an old saucepan or paint kettle. Pour smoothly in a thin stream into the filling hole until visible in the breather hole : fill to the top and allow to cool. When cold, separate the mould halves and check the casting for flaws. Cut off the two cores and remove the flash ; check weight and truth. Clean up with a worn file and old emery. Flat faces can be planed with an ordinary plane if lubricated with turpentine.

Fit the lead accurately to the deadwood (the remainder of the fin) which must, of course, be drilled for the bolts.

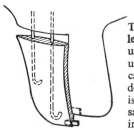

FIG. 108.

The heel of the lead, if of the usual pattern in use, must be located with the deadwood, which is best done by sawing a slit and inserting a slip of brass or similar, retaining this in place by copper rivets through lead and timber. Before permanently assembling, varnish the timber faces two or three coats, and varnish the lead faces immediately before clamping together. Any discrepancy arising through cleaning up or reducing weight should be made up with a slip of timber between the lead and the wood during assembly.

Plate-and-bulb keels have the bulb cast in two halves which are bolted through the fin (Fig. 109). Left-hand and right-hand patterns are required, of course.

The skeg of the boat was built in during the hull construction, and must now be fitted with the rudder trunk. This is a length of brass tube extending from slightly above deck level to the bottom of the skeg; where it emerges from the canoe body the rear half of the tube is removed by sawing (Fig. 110). The rear of the skeg should be channelled to receive the tube, and the tube positioned after varnishing or painting the channel. Small pins may be used to secure the cut-away part of the tube, but the heads must be filed away to leave a smooth bearing for the rudder stock.

The stock is a length of tube fitting snugly in the trunk, and the rudder is

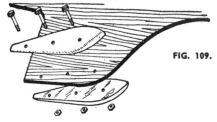

FIG. 109.

screwed to it (Fig. 111), the screwheads being filed away afterwards. A small plate screwed to the bottom of the skeg makes the lower bearing, either by having a pintle soldered in, engaging the stock, or being drilled to receive a pin fitted in the stock (Fig. 112). At the upper end, the stock must be long enough to provide fixing for the Braine quadrant or vane tiller; the best means of doing this is to sweat a threaded plug in the tube (Fig. 113).

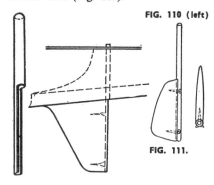

FIG. 110 (left)

FIG. 111.

A similar rudder arrangement may be employed for a full-keel boat (Fig. 103), but in the model world this type of keel is rapidly becoming obsolescent.

Inside the hull there is usually only one major fitting, the mast step. The mast of a yacht is adjustable fore and

FIG. 112.

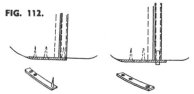

aft, both in position and in rake, in order that the finished yacht may be trimmed to the absolute limit of performance, and the mast step provides part of this adjustment. The heel of the mast is fitted with a tongue which engages one of several slots in the step (Fig. 114) to choice. For smaller yachts, the step can be cut from part of a piece of brass curtain rail (Fig. 115), but for larger boats it is built up from a strip

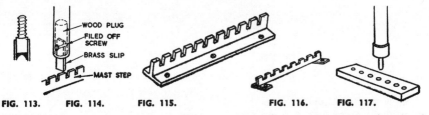

FIG. 113.   FIG. 114.   FIG. 115.   FIG. 116.   FIG. 117.

of heavy-gauge brass to which are silver-soldered feet (Fig. 116). The step is screwed directly to the backbone.

Small yachts can use a slightly different system. A peg is provided by screwing a cup-hook into the mast heel and sawing off. This peg engages one of several holes drilled in a strip of ply glued on deck, obviating a mast slide.

The mast slide is the second adjustment on the mast position and rake, and consists of a plate sliding in a tray (Fig. 118). A ferrule hard soldered to the plate accepts the mast, and holes are provided in both plate and tray to receive a pin, locking the plate in position. The tray is screwed in place on the deck, beams being positioned beneath, and a slot is cut in the deck to correspond with the slot in the tray.

Present-day practice is to make the mast of dural tube, where the rules allow, wood being used infrequently. Various methods of rigging a large model's mast are shown in Fig. 119, the best being, of course, the simplest (C) since this adequately braces the mast with the minimum of windage. Stainless steel wire is first choice for such rigging, except on small models, where braided flax or linen thread is acceptable. For wire, bottle-screws or turnbuckles are used to tighten up, but with thread bowsie adjustment is sufficient (Fig. 120).

A metal mast comprises a length of alloy tube ($\frac{3}{8}$ in. or $\frac{1}{2}$ in. Birmabright is the usual material), fitted with a tapered wooden top, and plugged at the lower end with dowel into which is fitted a metal tongue to engage the mast step (Fig. 114). A tapered tube is a refinement, and some metal fishing rod or aerial sections will provide such a tube, which obviates the need for a wood top. Metal spreader and jumper struts, etc., are best soldered to mast bands which slip over the mast snugly and can be held in place by a single bolt right through (Fig. 121), or clamped with a small bolt (Fig. 122).

A jackstay is usually fitted down the after side of the mast; this again is

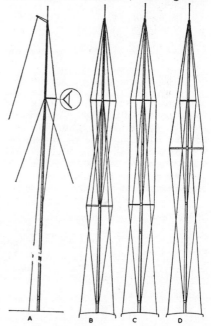

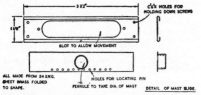

FIG. 118.—Dimensions in this and other figures are examples for a 10 R yacht. Right, **FIG. 119.**

A   B   C   D

FIG. 120.—Left to right, wire bowsies, flat and circular bowsies, turnbuckle, and bottle screw with left and right hand threads.

stainless steel wire, and is passed through eyes fitted to the mast and soldered to a screw or bolt top and bottom. It must be really taut. The eyes can be small screw-eyes with a wood mast, or split pins for a metal mast, fitted as Fig. 123.

Booms are usually cut and planed from timber, as in Fig. 124. Thin brass

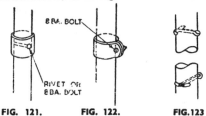

FIG. 121.   FIG. 122.   FIG.123.

bands are fitted round at points of attachment of eyes, etc., to prevent splitting or pulling out of the eyes. The main boom fits to the mast by means of a gooseneck, detailed in Fig. 125. The jib is permanently bent to its boom, so

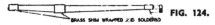

FIG. 124.

that separate booms are required for each suit of sails. Figs. 126 and 127 show a typical rigging set-up for both booms. The two types of bowsie (or bowser) used, with the correct methods of reeving them, are shown in Fig. 128.

When a boat is sailing, the wind pressure tends to belly the sail and lift

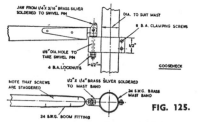

FIG. 125.

the boom. For running this is acceptable, since it cushions gusts which might otherwise cause the boat to luff. On other courses, however, it is a disadvantage and a kicking strap is therefore fitted to hold the boom down. This is usually strong line with an elastic insert, and is fitted with a bowsie for adjustment, i.e., slackening off for running, etc. (Fig. 129).

The remainder of the deck fittings consist of a jib rack, two horses, two chain-plates, and sundry eyes, etc., depending on the type of steering gear fitted. The jib rack (Fig. 130) resembles the mast step except that it incorporates

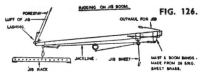

FIG. 126.

holes instead of slots, and can be made in a similar way. Horses are transverse rails to which the sheets are attached, and are usually constructed of brass wire, 16 s.w.g. for small models, up to 12 s.w.g. for large. Stops are provided at each end of the horizontal rail to prevent fouling at the corners, particularly in small sizes where the sheet ends in a hook engaged in the rail (Fig. 131).

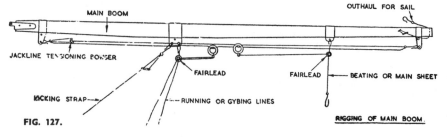

FIG. 127.

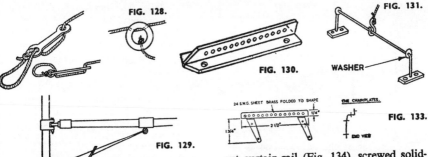

FIG. 128.

FIG. 130.

FIG. 131.

WASHER

FIG. 129.

24 S.W.G. SHEET BRASS FOLDED TO SHAPE

1/4"

1 3/4"

2 1/2"

THE CHAINPLATES.

FIG. 133.

END VIEW

Larger models employ travellers incorporating small rollers (Fig. 132).

The chain-plates are fitted on the boat's gunwales slightly aft of the mast, and take a considerable strain from the

cut curtain-rail (Fig. 134), screwed solidly to the inwale. Eyes are usually in the form of eye-plates, as in Fig. 135.

There are two basic steering mechanisms, the Braine and the vane gear. Their function is not to steer the boat

12 S.W.G. PHOS.BR. WIRE

5/8"

4 1/2"

4"

TRAVELLER

20 S.W.G. BRASS FEET DRILLED FOR SCREWS

HORSE.

FIG. 132.

FIG. 135.

FIG. 134.

shrouds. Consequently they must be very firmly secured, and on large models reinforcing straps are run down the side of the hull (Fig. 133) to distribute the strain. Small models can, again, use

on a predetermined course, but to keep the sails at a constant angle to the wind. The sails are trimmed for the required course, and the steering gear enables the boat to make the best of its trim.

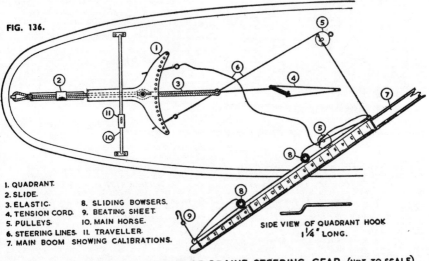

FIG. 136.

1. QUADRANT.
2. SLIDE.
3. ELASTIC.
4. TENSION CORD.
5. PULLEYS.
6. STEERING LINES.
7. MAIN BOOM SHOWING CALIBRATIONS.
8. SLIDING BOWSERS.
9. BEATING SHEET.
10. MAIN HORSE.
11. TRAVELLER.

SIDE VIEW OF QUADRANT HOOK
1 1/4" LONG.

DIAGRAMMATIC LAYOUT OF BRAINE STEERING GEAR (NOT TO SCALE)

FIG. 137.

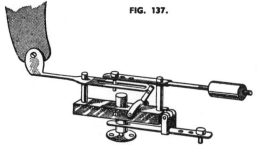

The simpler of the two systems is the Braine gear, which has been used for over forty years, and which is still popular for smaller craft. Fig. 136 is virtually self-explanatory. A quadrant fitted to the rudder stock is linked to the main boom as shown, and is tensioned by means of a rubber band attached to its tail. The tension of this band is normally adjustable for differing conditions by means of a slide. The boat is set off on its course and will continue until some condition causes it to come up to or fall off the wind. In the first case, the jib should bring it back on course, but if it falls off, the pressure on the mainsail will increase, overcoming the tension on the quadrant and turning the quadrant, thus giving corrective rudder. The degree of correction is adjustable by moving the sheets across the quadrant; it is important that both sheets are identical in length, so that the boat's behaviour is identical on either tack.

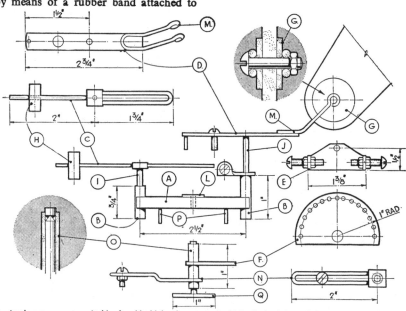

A simple vane gear, suitable for Marbleheads, etc. A. Main Body (channel brass ⅛ in. square). B. End Bearings (⅛ in. i.d. brass tube). C. Compensation Arm (brass rod 1/16 in. dia. threaded for weight—H). D. Vane Arm (brass strip 1/16 in. x ⅜ in.). E. Quadrant 1/32 in. brass with 6 BA nut soldered each end to take 6 BA bolts for adjusting length of tack. F. Main Quadrant (1/16 in. brass drilled 1/16 in. holes). G. Aluminium Discs (2 off for supporting vane with 6 BA bolt passing through). H. Lead Weight, threaded for adjustment. I, J. Brass spindles for vane arm and compensating arm (⅛ in. brass). K. Brass Pin 1/16 in. diameter to engage compensating arm C when self-tacking. L. Brass Plate soldered on top of open channel and drilled to take tube O. M. Brass Rod 1/16 in. diameter soldered to D and doubled to take vane. N. Vane Tiller 1/16 in. brass doubled and soldered to tube O. 6 BA bolt and nut fitted in gap and movable. O. Main Vane Bearing—brass tube with stub of ⅛ in. rod soldered in top. Main spindle of ⅛ in. brass fits in tube—top of spindle pointed to make needle bearing. P. Two 1/16 in. Brass Pins to engage in holes in main quadrant F. Q. Main Base of ⅛ in. brass with main spindle threaded and soldered on. See photos, Plate VII.

Several types of vane gear exist, but by far the most common is the Lassel pin-and-slot type shown in principle in Fig. 137. The vane feather (usually balsa) has an area of approximately five times the rudder area, and operates the rudder through a linkwork which generally incorporates a vane arm roughly twice as long as the tiller arm. A light rubber band tends to centre the vane in the same way as the Braine quadrant. Freedom of all moving parts and careful balance of the assembly are essential for successful operation, since where the Braine gear has the full power of the mainsail to move the rudder, this work must be done by the feather of the vane mechanism.

The usual gear has an adjustable self-tacking action which will produce the same angle of feather on each tack, or which can be set to sail the boat freer on one tack if desired. The gear is first balanced (in the water, because of rudder buoyancy) by sliding the counterweight to the appropriate position. It is then removed and the boat trimmed to sail a beat, with a locked rudder, so that it slowly works up into wind. The gear is refitted, set on the centre-line, and the self-tacking screws adjusted until the feather lines up with the apparent wind—about 30° to the centre line is normal. The idea is, obviously, is that when the wind blows the feather against either screw, the pressure will automatically apply corrective rudder. Adjustment of the screws will affect the boat's ability to hold a course close to the wind, and a little experimentation will soon demonstrate the correct setting.

For running, the self-tacking mechanism is locked and the gear rotated till the feather points forward. Again, experiment will soon determine the setting. The self-tacking gear is also locked for all other courses, the vane being lined up with the apparent wind. (N.B.—"Apparent" wind is the resultant between the true wind and the

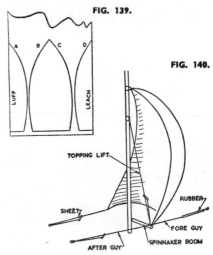

FIG. 139.

FIG. 140.

speed and direction of the boat.)

Visiting clubs and talking to members is the finest way to learn the tricks of vane operation, but the foregoing gives the basic principles of this ingenious gear.

Finally, sails. The sails are the driving force of a yacht and require to be very meticulously made. Most racing skippers have their sails made for them professionally, but briefly, the following procedure is used.

For smaller models, nurse's veiling or lightweight Egyptian cotton are suitable. Larger models use Egyptian cotton, Union silk, or varnished Terylene. Very

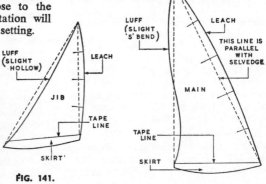

FIG. 141.

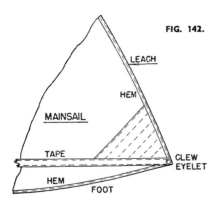

FIG. 142.

LOOSE FOOTED MAINSAIL HEMMED
FOOT & LEACH WITH REINFORCED
CORNER & EYELET

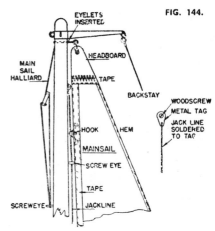

FIG. 144.

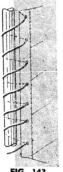

FIG. 143.

light sails, spinnakers, etc., are usually made from polythene. Fig. 139 shows how to cut a polythene spinnaker; the seams are cemented and sewn.

Paper patterns for the sails are an excellent idea, since they can be laid on the cloth to effect economy, besides being less expensive if cut wrong at first! The leaches of the sails *must* be parallel with the selvedge of the cloth, and the cloth must be pinned on a board perfectly flat but not stretched in any way, ready for cutting. Fig. 141 shows the shapes to be cut, rather exaggerated; the "S" bend on the luff should deviate from the straight by a minute amount—⅛ in. in a 50 in. luff. Allowance is made for as tiny a hem as can be sewn on leach and skirt, using light tension and fairly wide stitches on the machine. Reinforcements are sewn into the corners as sketched (Fig. 142).

The luff is sewn into a linen tape which is creased beforehand. Since the tape will eventually stretch more than the sail cloth it should be slightly shorter than the luff (only experience with the particular materials in use will show by how much), and the sail must be fed into the taut tape so that a series of tiny, evenly-spaced creases appear. These will stretch out as the sail is broken in. A length of tape is also sewn in a straight line from tack to clew. At the head of the sail, a short length of tape is sewn to reinforce the headboard attachment. The headboard is cut from ivorine or ply, etc., and sewn in place.

Batten pockets of sail cloth are sewn at right angles to the leach, as the rules allow, and stiff plastic or thin cane battens inserted before sewing up. The sails are completed by providing eyelets, if spiral lacing is to be used (Fig. 143), or hooks for attachment to the jackstay. These hooks are opened-out dressmakers' rustless hooks, eyeletted or sewn in place (Fig. 144). Eyelets must also be positioned at tack and clew of both sails, and at the jib head, for bending.

Serious sailing enthusiasts always have three suits of sails per yacht, since it is not possible to reef down a model yacht's sails without destroying their efficiency. The second suit normally has a total area of approximately 80 per cent of the top suit, and the third suit a total area of roughly 60 per cent. The sails are identical in every other respect.

Chapter Nine **Finishing**

MODELS can be made or marred by the quality of their paintwork, and it is well worth spending a good deal of time on this aspect of building. Care and cleanliness are essential to a good job—plus, of course, the patience required in rubbing down and waiting for successive coats to dry.

The inside of any boat must be waterproof, since some water is bound to find its way in, and inadequately protected wood will swell when soaked, and shrink when drying out. The least that can be expected from this is interference with the exterior paintwork and, at worst, it can completely ruin the model. Rubbing down inside is not an easy proposition, but if clean brushes and correctly mixed paint or varnish are used, and the interior is thoroughly and completely dusted before each coat, a very passable result can usually be achieved.

Varnish is the normal primer, but gold size is equally good. The first coat should be thinned half and half, and thoroughly brushed into every part ; the second also needs to be thin, though not quite to the extent of the first. From four to six coats of straight varnish should now be applied with a soft brush, working from a varnish tin stood in a bowl of hot water to keep the varnish runny. Between coats the brush should be thoroughly washed out in turpentine or white spirit, and washed under a running tap with a detergent. A final coat of cream or stone enamel will brighten the interior.

The outside should now be rubbed down and prepared for painting. If your building didn't quite come up to expectations and a couple of cracks or so are visible, these can be filled with paste driers or cellulose stopper, the former being preferable for a bright varnish (i.e., natural colour) hull. An alternative, especially where a fair number of fine gaps require attention, is to mix whiting with linseed oil and add a little drier, to make a thin putty-like substance. Leave the stopped hull till thoroughly dry, then rub down with fine glasspaper and dust off thoroughly.

Varnish, thinned 50-50 with pure turpentine, should now be brushed on as a primer, and rubbed down with fine paper when dry. A bright varnished hull must then receive five or six further coats of varnish, applied warm, and thoroughly rubbed down between each as in the following procedure for painting.

Use a good quality undercoat, and brush on one coat slightly thinned, over the varnish primer. Rub down with very fine glasspaper, dust off, and apply a second coat, also fairly thin (never use thick coats). Rub down with No. 320 "wet-or-dry" paper ; this is a carborundum-dust paper bonded to a waterproof backing, obtainable at motor accessory dealers or reputable ironmongers. The rate of cutting down with this paper, used wet, is remarkable. Sponge over, dry off thoroughly, and apply another coat. Repeat this procedure until a completely smooth surface, free of any imperfections, is

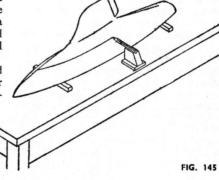

FIG. 145

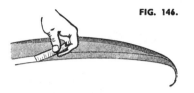

FIG. 146.

evident after sponging; probably a further three to four coats will be necessary with normal timber grain.

Now brush on a coat of finishing enamel, again slightly thinned. Use a perfectly clean brush and brush the colour out well. Allow to dry and rub down with No. 400 paper. Apply a second coat, and again rub down. The final coat can be fairly well thinned, rubbed over with metal polish, and brought to a high gloss with a wax car polish.

Always use a perfectly clean brush and ensure that the paint is thoroughly mixed and strained through two thicknesses of nylon stocking tied over the mouth of a clean tin. Leave the hull in a dust-free room to dry off, particularly for the enamel coats.

Most hulls are painted in two colours, and the above procedure should be followed except that only one colour at a time is applied, the colour line being masked off to obtain a really neat edge. To determine the correct waterline, mark it off at bow and stern (from the plan or from flotation tests), and block the hull upside-down on the bench so that the points marked are an equal distance above the bench. Mount a pencil, crayon, or stick of chalk sharpened to a chisel edge on a block of appropriate height, and draw the waterline lightly in by sliding the block round the hull (Fig. 145). The mask is a strip of adhesive tape positioned accurately to this line; cellophane tape is perfectly suitable provided that the edge is sealed by running a spoon along to press it firmly down, but with some paints it must be removed with care, by doubling the end back and drawing it off gently (Fig. 146), to avoid lifting the paint. A surer but more tedious job is to use gummed brown paper strip, which must be soaked off.

For best results, the mask should be reapplied for each coat, i.e., with a white and red hull the first coat of white should be brushed on, then the mask removed and the first coat of red applied after masking the white. The whole hull is then rubbed down, and the red re-masked for the second coat of white, and so on. This ensures a smooth paint scheme with no ridge along the colour-line.

Decks are normally finished before fitting, since it is easier to line them separately. Occasionally a yacht deck is painted white or ivory before lining, but the procedure is very similar. Ply is frequently too light in colour for a true representation of mahogany or teak planking, so after varnishing the underside several coats the upperside must be stained. Spirit or water-stain is suitable, and a small quantity should be mixed thin and tried on a scrap of material. Several thin coats will result in a more even colour than one thick one. When the desired hue is achieved, leave to dry thoroughly before applying a coat of varnish primer. Rub down and apply two more coats, rubbing down with 400 paper. Check that a pencil mark can be erased; if not, apply a further coat.

The classic deck lay-out for a yacht is shown in Fig. 147; the king-plank and cover-boards are frequently coloured slightly darker after lining, using scumble or some similar oil-stain, or wood-dye. Planking for a scale type deck will be on the lines shown in Fig. 148. Remember that full-size planking rarely exceeds 6 in. in width, and is frequently only 3 in. or 4 in.; work out a roughly scale width for your particular model.

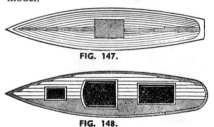

FIG. 147.

FIG. 148.

Mark out the planking with clear pencil lines; a simple tool such as that in Fig. 149 will facilitate this. When the marking out is satisfactory, dust the deck lightly with french chalk to "kill" any grease, and ink the lines over with Indian ink, using a ruling pen. Use a smooth spline about ⅛ in. square to rule the curves—this is one job where an assistant is useful. Note that the planks are irregularly joggled into the king-plank and/or waterways. Smudges or slips should be allowed to dry, then lightly scraped away with a razor blade. Colour king-plank, etc., if desired.

When dry, dust off, and apply another coat of varnish. Rub down with 400 paper, and repeat. Flow the last coat on fairly thickly (i.e., don't brush out *quite* so much) and leave the deck truly horizontal in a completely dust-free room for forty-eight hours.

Wood masts and spars look extremely elegant if french polished before varnishing. Cabin tops, etc., may also receive similar treatment. The grain of the wood should first be filled by rubbing in a plaster of paris paste; wipe off with a damp rag and when set rub down with worn fine glasspaper. The plaster must now be "killed" with raw linseed oil; wipe off and apply a coat of polish, allow to dry and apply four or five more. Polish up with methylated spirit on a tuft of cotton wool, or varnish two coats.

Painted superstructure requires similar treatment to the hull, using masking where necessary. Small parts and fittings are best painted before assembly where possible.

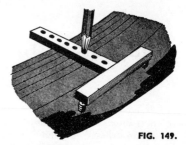

FIG. 149.

Some builders find difficulty in choosing a colour scheme for their boats, particularly launch or small cruiser types. The majority of these are painted white above the waterline, and use green, red, or bronze coloured anti fouling paint below. Superstructures ar most often varnished, decks natural planking, and tops stone or buff colour Many boats in unsheltered moorings have canvas or linoleum covered tops, painted buff. Ports, handrails, etc., are usually polished brass, other fittings bronze or brass, or painted aluminium, red oxide, or sometimes black, wearing silvery where ropes rub. Well interiors are brown or natural varnish, cabin interiors white or cream with varnished fittings.

Some readers may be surprised that so much trouble over painting is recommended, but the paintwork can make or mar a model's appearance, and when so much time and trouble have gone into the construction, and the model may be expected to give some years of service, an extra hour or two in giving it a proper, durable finish can hardly be considered wasted.

Chapter Ten

Internal Combustion Engines

THERE is little doubt that the modern miniature "diesel" is equalled only by electric motors in popularity as a power plant for model boats. Originally designed for use in model aircraft, the diesel was rapidly adapted to marine work and now most manufacturers include marine versions of their motors in their ranges. Since a considerable number of aeromodellers also indulge in boating, marine conversion units are available; alternatively, most engines intended for aircraft use can be adapted for boats with little difficulty by builders themselves.

A typical normal modern motor is sketched in Fig. 150. For the complete novice, it should be mentioned that there are three basic types of induction—sideport, disc, and crankshaft (rotary), (Fig. 151), the last of which is now in most widespread use. All diesels are two-stroke, i.e., mixture is drawn into the crankcase as the piston rises and moves into the cylinder via transfer passages as the piston descends. The fuel varies with different motors for peak performance,

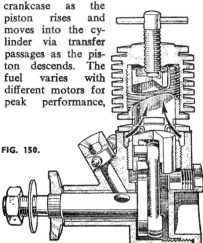

FIG. 150.

but almost without exception diesels will run on equal parts of ether, paraffin, and castor oil.

Maximum power is developed at fairly high r.p.m.—something in the nature of 10,000-12,000—and with normal diesel direct-drive installations this means a fairly small propeller with small blade area and pitch (q.v.). A flywheel is essential for starting and running, and the motor must be rigidly and strongly mounted in the hull.

FIG. 151.—Sideport, crankshaft, and disc induction.

Most modern motors are provided with lugs on each side of the crankcase for fixing (beam mount), but occasionally radial mounting is employed, when the motor is provided with a crankcase backplate for clamping to a ply structural member (Fig. 152). The simplest method of beam mounting is to fit a shelf athwart the boat, with a cut-out for the motor seating. The shelf may be of $\frac{3}{16}$ in. or thicker ply, or 14 s.w.g. brass sheet, etc., and must be firmly bolted or screwed to blocks glued and screwed into the main structure (Fig. 153); the motor is bolted in its seating, using spring washers and lock-nuts to avoid loosening due to vibration. Alternatively, a short shelf may be used, screwed to cheeks which are bolted, with appropriate spacing blocks, through the keel (Fig. 154). Other methods are sketched in Fig. 155.

To arrive at the correct position for the motor itself, several factors must be

FIG. 152.

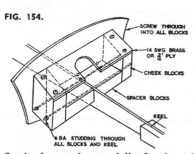

FIG. 154.

SCREW THROUGH INTO ALL BLOCKS

14 SWG BRASS OR ¾" PLY

CHEEK BLOCKS

SPACER BLOCKS

KEEL

6 BA STUDDING THROUGH ALL BLOCKS AND KEEL

considered. The propeller shaft should be as nearly horizontal as possible, the limiting factors being clearance for the propeller at one end and the flywheel at the other. It is not advisable to use a shaft of more than about 12 in. length, since this produces whip and introduces bearing complications. Once the shaft tube is in place, the complete assembly should be made up to assist in determining the exact position of the motor ; after fixing the mounting, small packing pieces can be used to bring the motor dead in line with the shaft.

Four factors must be considered in the flywheel—weight, diameter, fitting, and truth. There is no need to exceed about 2¼ in. flywheel diameter for any motor under 10 c.c., and an average weight of about 5 oz. can be used for any motor of from 2-5 c.c. (See App. VI). Weight is not critical, as some modellers believe, it merely affects the time taken for the motor to reach maximum r.p.m., and it is better to err on the too-heavy side. The distribution of the weight is important, and it should be concentrated on the periphery of the wheel as in Fig. 156. Modern motors nearly all use a tapered crankshaft for locking, and the

flywheel must be carefully fitted to this. Alternatively, a keyway must be cut in the crankshaft, and a silver steel key inserted (Fig. 157).

The most important factor is truth, for an out-of-balance flywheel will wear the crankshaft bearings oval in minutes, thus losing crankcase compression and reducing the efficiency (and finally ruining) the motor. Flywheels are commercially available to fit just about every known motor, and the builder is urged to buy one from a reputable firm rather than make do with something improvised. These flywheels are all provided with a peripheral groove or an integral pulley for starting purposes, and if you are able accurately to turn your own, something of this nature should be incorporated.

There are several methods of connecting the flywheel to the propeller shaft for driving. A certain amount of flexibility is essential, and there are on the market several flexible or universal couplings which are admirable. The simplest of these consists of two knurled fittings provided with hexagonal tips and threaded, one for the engine crankshaft (also holding the flywheel in place) and one for the shaft. A length of thick

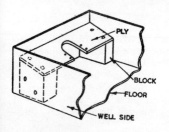

PLY

BLOCK

FLOOR

WELL SIDE

FIG. 153.

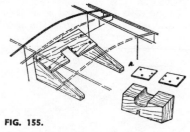

FIG. 155.

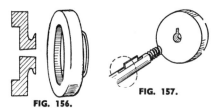

FIG. 157.

FIG. 156.

neoprene tube is pushed over the knurls to make an ideal and virtually permanent coupling (Fig. 158). Another method of doing the same job is to hard solder a few turns of a stout spring between two collars screwing on the shafts (Fig. 159).

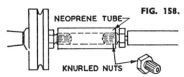

FIG. 158.

NEOPRENE TUBE

KNURLED NUTS

More mechanical is the universal shown in Fig. 160, consisting of two threaded collars shaped at their meeting ends and pinned through each other. Fig. 161 shows a dog method ; one or two silver steel pins extending from the

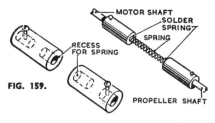

MOTOR SHAFT
SOLDER SPRING
SPRING
RECESS FOR SPRING

FIG. 159.

PROPELLER SHAFT

flywheel face located in notches in a driven disc fitted to the shaft. A simple clutch giving friction drive is detailed in Fig. 162.

The propeller shaft should be of stainless steel, at least $\frac{1}{8}$ in. dia. The usual practice is to instal it in a brass tube giving at least $\frac{1}{32}$ in. clearance all round,

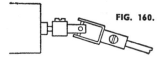

FIG. 160.

with a reamed brass or bronze bush about $\frac{1}{8}$ in. in length pressed into each end. Warm vaseline is sucked up into the tube and allowed to solidify before finally pushing the shaft through, and sometimes a greasing hole is drilled on top, at the top end, into which melted vaseline can be poured from time to time. The grease stops water from working its way up.

FIG. 161.

Occasionally a stuffing box (Fig. 163) is used, with an exposed shaft. This is usually confined to hydroplanes where the hull is not really in the water during operation. Little water finds its way up the tube, in any event, if the

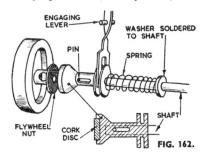

ENGAGING LEVER
WASHER SOLDERED TO SHAFT
PIN
SPRING
FLYWHEEL NUT
CORK DISC
SHAFT

FIG. 162.

shaft fit is good. The advantages are less resistance and ease of fitting a universal ; the propeller thrust must be horizontal on very high speed models, to prevent nosing under.

FIG. 163.

Propellers for diesels are usually two-bladed, since there is power to spare and the disadvantages of two blades lessen with high rotational speeds. Suitable props for various motors are given in Appendix VI, but a brief explanation of pitch, etc., may not be amiss here. Pitch

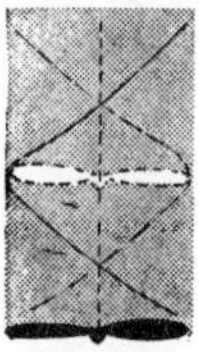

FIG. 164.

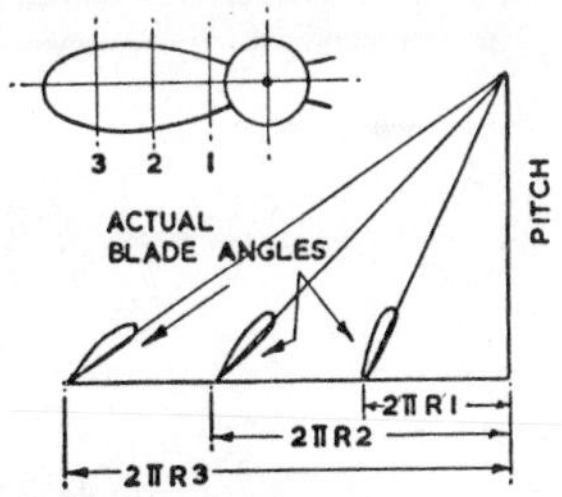

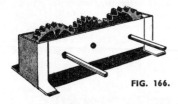

FIG. 165.

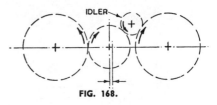

FIG. 168.

is the theoretical distance moved forward by the propeller (or screw) in one complete revolution (Fig. 164). In actual fact, propeller slip occurs and the actual distance moved is approximately 60 per cent of the theoretic pitch.

It will be seen that to design a propeller for maximum efficiency the boat's speed must be estimated, plus the working r.p.m. of the motor. A small calculation will give the theoretical pitch

This simplifies attachment, since a normal thread can be used, the water resistance tending to tighten it on the shaft.

Some advantage is gained in "conventional" boats by using a large three-blade propeller driven at slower speed by gearing the motor down. Unfortunately, the mechanical losses in the gears cancel out the increased efficiency of the screw in the case of small i.c. engines, so there is little point in employing gears unless twin screws are required. In such a case,

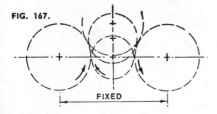

FIG. 166.

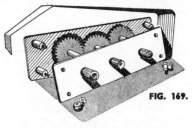

FIG. 169.

required, from which it is simple to arrive at the actual pitch. The blade angle can be approximated from a geometric drawing such as Fig. 165. Diameters are normally half to three-quarters of the theoretic pitch; blade area must be adjusted until the working r.p.m. estimated are obtained.

There is no difference in the performance of propellers of either hand, and with virtually all motors nowadays rotating anti-clockwise (viewed from astern) a left-hand prop. will be needed.

a gearbox or frame will be necessary, and advantage may very well be taken of the benefits of reduction gearing.

Quite a number of successful boats employ an open gear frame (Fig. 166) with no lubrication system, and some even use brass gears. For long life, however, it pays to invest in steel spur gears, and run their shafts through bronze bushes hard soldered to the frame. A touch of grease now

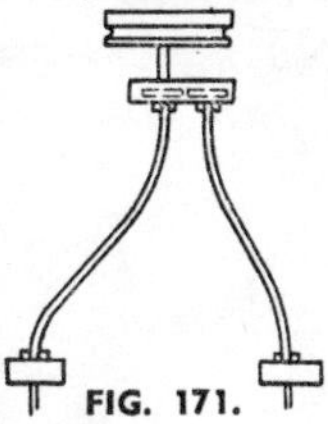

FIG. 167.

FIXED

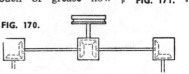

FIG. 170.

FIG. 171.

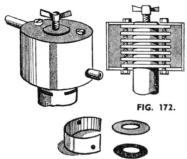

FIG. 172.

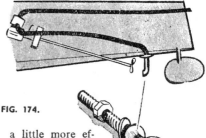

FIG. 174.

and then will ensure smoother and quieter running. The gear diameters required can quickly be assessed by drawing out the shaft spacing, etc., as in Fig. 167. For contra-rotating shafts an idler gear will be necessary, and this means mounting the motor just far enough off centre to enable the idler to be dropped in (Fig. 168).

Enclosed gear-boxes tend to become a little unwieldy with wide-spaced shafts, but are quite common. Fig. 169 illustrates a simple and reasonably lightweight method of construction. Alternative drives are a double bevel arrangement with three boxes (Fig. 170), though this is rather expensive (7 bevels!) and absorbs considerable power, or a flex drive system as sketched in Fig. 171, which is put forward as an entirely feasible idea for small motors, but one which, as far as is known, has not yet been tried.

The question of cooling a motor is a relatively easy one. Actually, sufficient cooling is achieved by heat dissipation through the fins of an aircraft motor if the head is well exposed to the air, but most motors run

a little more efficiently if kept really cool, and in recent years water jackets have become virtually universal. Jackets can be purchased for most motors, or the motors bought ready-fitted, but conversion is not a difficult job with the average engine. The fins are unscrewed and appropriate copper or brass discs fitted top and bottom, held by three or four bolts passed right through the fins. A little sealing composition beneath the discs, or rubber washers, etc., can be used if desired. A strip of thin copper or brass is now soft-soldered round the discs, and stub tubes fitted top and bottom (Fig. 172).

This or any other water jacket, can be cooled in two ways. Fig. 173 shows convection cooling, in which a header tank containing water is mounted above the motor. The usual system, however, relies on the water through which the boat moves, collecting it by means of a scoop and returning it over the side when it has passed the engine. If the scoop is placed immediately aft of the propeller (Fig. 174) water is forced through the jacket even when the boat is

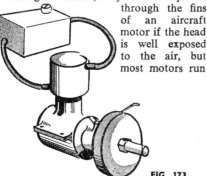

FIG. 173.

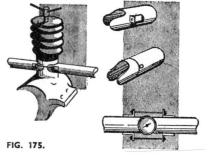

FIG. 175.

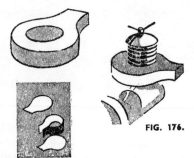

FIG. 176.

bolted to each other by means of lugs or twisted wires soldered to the tubes. Many modern 360° ported motors can be fitted with a manifold as in Fig. 176, large bore neoprene or rubber tube be-

held stationary, and is ejected with astonishing power from the outlet. Neoprene tubing is used to connect scoop and outlet to the jacket.

The exhaust from the engine is messy and oily, and should be led away outside if possible. It is important to remember that at no point should the cross-section of the exhaust pipe be less than the total area of the engine's exhaust port(s), otherwise back-pressure will be built up, seriously reducing the engine's power. Where an exhaust cannot be bolted to the engine, the device shown in Fig. 175 can be used; thin brass or copper tubes are cut and filed to fit round the cylinder barrel, over the exhaust ports, and

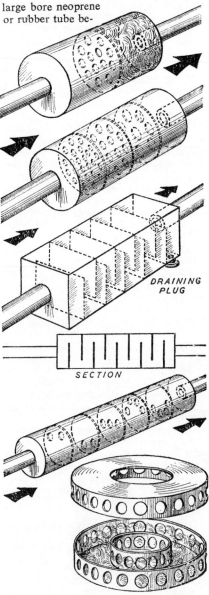

DRAINING PLUG

SECTION

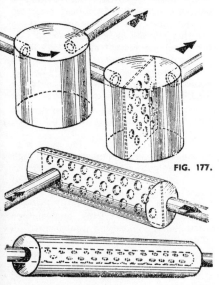

FIG. 177.

ing used to connect up the exhaust pipe.

Something which is becoming more important as more boats take the water is the question of silencing. Silencers are easily constructed (they must be hard soldered), and a selection of types is shown in Figs. 177 and 178. The idea is simply to break up the high-frequency sound waves before allowing them to escape. Many local authorities make silencing mandatory, and it is foolish to lose the use of a stretch of water because of noise nuisance when the remedy is so easy.

Finally, a thought about tanks. The tank should be mounted as close to the engine as possible, with the fuel level at approximately the same height as the engine needle valve for easy starting. Fuel surge may become important in a high speed, highly manoeuvrable boat, and baffles are sometimes used to obviate this. Fig. 179 shows the best type of tank for high speed work.

Petrol Engines

Petrol engines are broadly similar to diesels in operation, etc., so that most of this chapter so far applies. The difference is, of course, that a petrol engine has an ignition system and sparking plug. The wiring is shown in Fig. 180, and the big point about it is that sound, clean, preferably soldered joints must be made throughout. It is also necessary to keep the ignition gear perfectly dry, and to ensure that fresh batteries or a fresh charged accumulator are used.

The main advantage of the petrol engine is its great flexibility, a speed range of 1,500-9,000 r.p.m. being quite normal. Nevertheless, these motors are popular only in large sizes—over 10 c.c.—and there are very few to be had nowadays.

Occasionally magneto ignition is used, and four-stroke units are seen. These

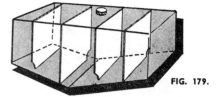

FIG. 179.

FEED ↓

are usually confined to racing enthusiasts able to construct their own motors, and only one ready to run four-stroke has been marketed in quantity in recent years ; it is still available.

Glowplug Engines

These engines are a sort of half-way mark between diesel and petrol. They employ the lighter construction of the petrol engine, but require no ignition equipment once started. Like diesels, the range over which the speed may be controlled is relatively small. The actual ignition is brought about by a plug which is rather similar to a sparking plug, but has a permanent element between the electrodes. When a battery is connected up, the element glows and the motor may be started. The battery is then disconnected and the heat generated at each combustion is enough to keep the plug glowing to ignite the next. Unfortunately, a methyl alcohol/castor oil fuel is necessary, and this is remarkably active against most paints and glues. A special fuel-proofer must therefore be used, but unless the utmost care is taken in its application, the fuel will penetrate and soak into the structure behind the proofer.

The special virtue of the glow-plug engine is its very high speed and high power output at high speeds. It is therefore particularly useful for speed work, and its chief application in the model boat world, at least in Europe, is for hydroplane racing and similar speed work. Glowplug motors can, of course, be used in any boat if care is taken over fuel-proofing, and the installation details already given apply in exactly the same way.

FIG. 180.

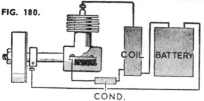

COIL   BATTERY

COND.

Chapter Eleven

Steam Engines

ONE of the cheapest power plants to run is the steam engine, and, of course, there is the added attraction of there being something scale about it. It has the disadvantages of being rather hot and messy to operate, and is rather heavy and bulky for the power produced; nevertheless, it is very fascinating and there are few other forms of power which can be started up to provide three or four hours non-stop cruising for the outlay of a few pence. There are two usual types of steam engine, the oscillator and the slide valve, but there are many variations in boilers and lamps, so it is perhaps advisable to examine them one by one.

Oscillating Engines

The name of these motors originates from the fact that the cylinder(s) oscillate(s) when the engine is running. Instead of the normal gudgeon pin fitting, the connecting rod is rigidly fixed to the piston, and as the crankshaft rotates the cylinder is rocked from side

FIG. 181.

to side. The back side of the cylinder is ground to a flat face which bears on a valve block, also flat-faced. The valve block is provided with inlet and exhaust ports with which the cylinder inlet and exhaust ports register (Fig. 181).

Because of the relatively simple construction, oscillating engines are usually inexpensive to buy, and will work off quite a low steam pressure, such as can be obtained from the simplest type of boiler. The simplicity is carried over to the lubrication system, which usually consists of a vertical oil container through which the steam passes on its way to the cylinder. Some of the steam condenses, sinks, and displaces oil which then flows into the cylinder.

Power output is not large, but will vary with the accuracy with which the engine is made, and the steam pressure.

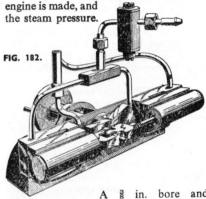

FIG. 182.

A ⅜ in. bore and stroke motor on 12-15 lb. pressure will on average provide sufficient power for a 24-30 in. model weighing approximately 4 lb.

Multi-cylinder oscillators can be built, most popular being the horizontally-opposed twin lay-out (Fig. 182). A 30-36 in. hull weighing about 8 lb. can be satisfactorily powered on 15 lb. steam with a ½ in. bore and stroke twin-cylinder engine.

Slide Valve Engines

The second type of steam engine widely used in all sizes of model from 30 in. up, is the more efficient slide-valve design. The piston arrangement is conventional and the cylinder fixed, but an eccentric is fitted to the crankshaft and operates a valve-rod connected to a slide moving in a valve-chest. The slide is milled out to allow passage of steam between two pairs of pipes as shown in Fig. 183. Steam losses are

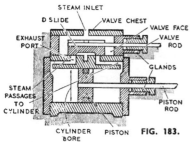

FIG. 183.

very slight compared with an oscillator, and slide-valve engines are generally considered to be more of an "engineering job", suited to serious work.

The power available from these engines is considerable, an example being a single cylinder, ¾ in. bore and stroke, working on 40-50 lb. pressure, which is quite adequate for a 4 ft. boat weighing about 45 lb. Multi-cylinder arrangements are quite common, the cylinders normally being in line.

Boilers

The simplest form of boiler is that shown in Fig. 184, consisting of a water container in a casing which allows sufficient room beneath for a burner, which may be a methylated spirit lamp or a small tray on which is burned a solid fuel such as *Meta*.

Developments of this are usually concentrated on improving the heat supply or lowering the overall height. The "chicken-feed" burner in Fig. 185

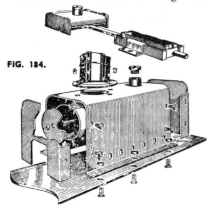

FIG. 184.

achieves both these ends, since it permits greater flame spread for the same duration with a shallower tank than Fig. 184, the means being an external supply tank for the spirit. Since the burner is of necessity as low in the boat as possible, the tank is higher than flame level, and to prevent flooding is made completely air-tight. By means of a pressure balance pipe and a small reservoir (Fig. 186), a steady drip-feed is maintained, in the manner of a chicken feeder hopper.

FIG. 185.

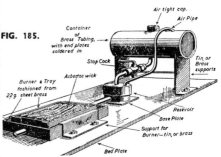

The next step in boiler efficiency is to increase the area of heating surface, and this is achieved in its simplest form by placing vertical tubes through the boiler, through which the heat passes (Fig. 187). Next, cross-tubes can be introduced (Fig.

FIG. 186.

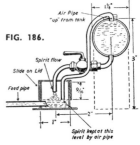

188), to allow the water to circulate through the flames. The culmination of these methods is the centre-flue boiler, in which a blowlamp flame is played through a tubular boiler equipped with cross-tubes (Fig. 189).

Specialists in steam work go in for real engineering practices, such as pump fed boilers and high efficiency units

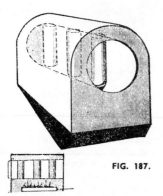

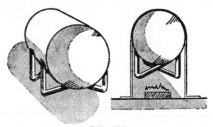

FIG. 188.

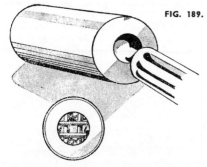

FIG. 187.

operating on the flash steam principle. In this system a series of pipes are heated almost red hot by one or more blowlamp flames, and water is fed in at a controlled rate. Needless to say its

FIG. 189.

vaporisation is instantaneous, and the volume of steam produced is quite extraordinary. Models powered with engines running off such boilers do in fact compare quite reasonably in speed with racing models powered by the more frequently encountered petrol engines. The subject, fascinating as it is, is just a little beyond the scope of this present book.

Any of the coupling methods described in the previous chapter are suitable for steam engines, but installation is a little different. By far the best system is to mount the entire boiler and engine assembly on a single aluminium or alloy plate, which can then be fitted into the hull by four single bolts. The surrounding woodwork should be painted with a heat-proof paint, or, in the region of extreme heat, it may be insulated with asbestos paper, attached using waterglass as an adhesive.

If radio is to be fitted, it must be an entirely separate unit, sealed off from heat, steam, water, oil, etc. It should be feasible to control a steam regulator to give a speed range, as well as normal steering control, but as far as is known this has never yet been done.

One feature of steam is that power output does not vary with r.p.m. to anything like the extent of diesels, and the r.p.m. available are considerably lower in any event. This means that a fairly large three-blade prop. can be used—as a very rough rule of thumb, 1 in. of diameter for every $\frac{1}{4}$ in. of engine bore. Gearing down is not normally necessary.

Chapter Twelve   Electric Motors

PROBABLY no range of motors offers the scope in power output available from electric motors. Miniature units weighing little more than 1 oz. can be used in boats as small as 8 in. in length, and at the other extreme are motors suitable for powering six and seven foot models. The most frequent use of electric power is in boats of less than 36 in. l.o.a., although many larger models use it for its cleanliness and ease of operation and control. In small sizes the expenditure in dry batteries is not a serious drawback, but large motors can be quite expensive unless re-chargeable accumulators are used, in which case the initial expense is fairly heavy, but the subsequent running costs negligible.

For maximum efficiency, an electric motor should drive a propeller through a reduction gear (except for speed models) since usually the most efficient running speed of any electric motor, in terms of power output and current drain, is at least three times the speed at which it could be expected to drive a useful propeller. Fortunately, for most installations, inexpensive brass gears are perfectly adequate, and, in fact, an old clock will frequently supply all that is necessary. Alternatively, belt-driven pulleys can be used with entirely satisfactory results, particularly where two shafts are taken from the same motor. Pulleys are available in many sizes, or can be turned up, or laminated from washers of differing diameters bolted or soldered to the shafts. Contra-rotation is easily arranged by crossing the appropriate belt, and no coupling troubles are likely to arise. If couplings are required, any of those in Chap. X are suitable, or the simplified arrangements shown in Fig. 190 may be used. Miniature motors will drive efficiently through

a length of insulation stripped off lighting flex and forced on the shafts.

The usual method of installation is to screw or bolt the motor to a block or blocks glued and screwed to the main structure. Washers may be used to pack the motor to the correct height; the couplings should run as truly as possible since power is wasted otherwise. Even when gears are used it pays to connect the motor to the drive gear with a flexible coupling, which reduces vibration and wear.

Wiring should be neat and firm, with soldered joints where possible. Care should be taken to keep the installation free of water and excess oil. It is customary to have a permanent switch built into the fixed superstructure, either placed as unobtrusively as possible, or disguised as a deck fitting such as a capstan.

Dry batteries should be stowed in permanent battery boxes such as that shown in Fig. 191. This facilitates easy replacement of the batteries, and also means that it is no trouble to take out unexpended batteries after a day's sailing; never leave batteries in in case they have been slightly dampened.

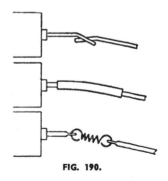

FIG. 190.

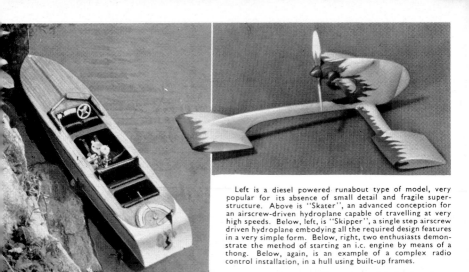

Left is a diesel powered runabout type of model, very popular for its absence of small detail and fragile superstructure. Above is "Skater", an advanced conception for an airscrew-driven hydroplane capable of travelling at very high speeds. Below, left, is "Skipper", a single step airscrew driven hydroplane embodying all the required design features in a very simple form. Below, right, two enthusiasts demonstrate the method of starting an i.c. engine by means of a thong. Below, again, is an example of a complex radio control installation, in a hull using built-up frames.

Below, left, an example of an outboard motor boat using an American .8 c.c. commercial glow-plug engine. Below, a sample of a standard commercial diesel fitted with water jacket and flywheel as standard items.

PLATE 5.

Above is a 15 c.c. petrol engine with water cooling and exhaust silencer; note that the water outlet is led into the exhaust tube aft of the silencer. Gear box forward of engine is R.C. ignition advance and retard mechanism. Right, a simple metal hull with radio gear in separate compartments and a novel tapered flywheel to assist in obtaining a shallow shaft angle. Below, a simple steam unit incorporating chicken feed burner.

Above, a Kitchen rudder installation. Below, left close-up of the horizontally opposed oscillating steam engine in the photograph above. Below is an example of the simplest type of water cooled diesel installation with flexible shaft coupling. The exhaust is free to fill the boat, and the cabin windows are unglazed to provide adequate ventilation.

PLATE 6.

Free acid batteries are sometimes used, and these must be stowed so that they are unable to spill. As a precaution, they should be carried in an entirely separate sealed-off compartment.

One of the most useful sources of inexpensive but powerful electric motors is the Government surplus stockist. Most of these motors were originally made for aircraft instruments, and are usually 24 v., though most give a very useful power output at 12 v. To supply such a voltage for long periods is extremely expensive with dry batteries, even if you can afford the space and weight of a large capacity block of, say, eight 1½ v. bell batteries, and it is usual to use small accumulators to supply the current for such motors. There are several makes of light weight accumulators available, any of which will give many hours of trouble-free running with an occasional charge. Cost varies from 30/- to £3 or so, and two may be needed; they will, however, give many years of service if looked after in accordance with the maker's instructions, and considering initial outlay, fuel costs, length of life, and general operating expenses, the electric motor plus accumulator power pack compares very favourably with other forms of power in cost per hour's operation.

It is extremely difficult to lay down any hard and fast rules as to the size of a boat any particular electric motor would propel, but under good conditions (i.e. an efficient screw with the engine working at its most efficient speed), a motor giving 1 in./ounce of torque when stalled will propel a boat up to 18 in. in length, weighing up to 10 oz., and a motor giving a stall torque of 3 in./oz. would give a satisfactory speed for a boat of about 36 in. l.o.a., and weighing up to, say, 8 lb. Stall torque figures for a wide range of British motors will be found in Appendix 7.

Propeller sizes will again depend on the efficient operating speed of the motor and the gear ratios used, but

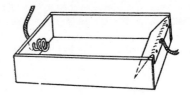

FIG. 191.

three-bladed screws are customary and may perhaps best be related to the length of the boat, an empirical figure being ¾ in. diameter per foot of hull length. Pitch should be calculated as on page 57.

The consumption of a nicely aligned motor in amps depends on the propeller, and the work it does is expressed in watts (amps x volts). Thus fitting a larger propeller and running off the same power supply increases power by increasing the amps drawn, shortening the time the current can be drawn from the power source. A very rule-of-thumb approach is to load the motor with a prop of a size which results in the motor being just warm to the touch after, say, a five-minute run; this normally means that the motor is working as hard as is consistent with reasonable life. A higher load shortens brush life and may overheat the motor to the point of seizure, or the windings can burn out. To propel a boat of, say, 30 ins. length and 5 lbs. weight at around walking speed will usually require something over 45 watts—12 v. at 4 amps or 6 v. at 8 amps —which can only be supplied satisfactorily by accumulators.

In general the speed attainable with electric power is much below that achieved with internal combustion engines, but on the other hand they are much less trouble to operate, and produce no nuisance in the form of noise or smell. Where speed is of secondary importance—as in many radio controlled models—the advantages of the electric motor are considerable.

Chapter Thirteen Hydroplanes and Special Models

ONE very popular form of water-borne modelling is the running of airscrew-driven hydroplanes. These are usually light and simple models, borrowing much from model aircraft techniques, and employing balsa and ply structures. They can be run free on isolated ponds, or tethered if very high speeds are desired ; it is quite possible to reach 70-75 m.p.h. with a 2½ c.c. diesel.

Design is aimed at producing a light planing hull usually employing a step, having sufficient beam to resist rolling

FIG. 192.

induced by torque. Directional stability is achieved by side area both above and below water, and longitudinal stability (pitch) is induced by providing a hull with a C.G. (centre of gravity) fairly well aft, the engine having slight down-thrust to hold the bow down, and the shape of the planing surface being arranged to provide up-thrust. Correct relation of these factors produces a damping effect which irons out pitching or porpoising. *Skipper* (Plate V) shows a successful typical model of this sort.

Racing Hydroplanes

As with any model designed for "ultimate performance", a racing model hydroplane demands considerable skill and patience to achieve good results. The modern craft of this type normally employs three point suspension, i.e., the model is in contact with the water at three small points only when at speed. These points are usually provided by the trailing tips of two sponsons at the bow (Fig. 193), and the extreme stern of the boat—a total area of a mere square inch or so.

FIG. 193.

A line is always used to tether the model to a fixed point, and so fast are some hydroplanes that the engines are designed to run at settings taking into account the spray drawn into the engine —spray still in the air from the previous circuit ! All-ply, all-metal, or mixed ply and metal construction may be used, and the static buoyancy is usually marginal, just enough to keep the boat on the surface.

An important factor in design is the shaft and screw arrangement. The screw thrust *must* be horizontal or the boat will dive or back-flip, and this means a second universal at the lower end of the shaft. Normally open shafts and stuffing boxes are used, as mentioned earlier, and the propeller is fitted in a bearing which is carried on a fitting variously known as an A-frame, skeg, or prop-bracket. This, of course, has to be a very rigid fitting, and is usually filed from a casting or from the solid, with

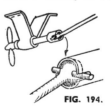

FIG. 194.

in the latter case the tube bearing and attachment lugs brazed on (Fig. 194). Props are usually only half immersed when running.

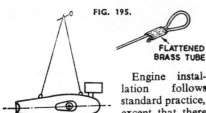

FIG. 195.

FLATTENED
BRASS TUBE

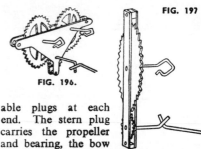

FIG. 196.

FIG. 197

Engine installation follows standard practice, except that there is rather less room than usual. Tanks for circular running are, of course, a different proposition, since centrifugal force will throw the fuel to the outside, and the effort required to suck fuel will vary with the quantity remaining in the tank. This is the reason for a hydroplane engine "peaking" or "coming in" at one point during the run. The feed pipe must obviously run to the outside rear corner of the tank, and high, narrow tanks reduce the sideways head of fuel when in motion. Experimentation is usually necessary to determine the best type of tank and its actual position.

Two-point attachment of the bridle is customary ; the fore-and-aft position of the line connection can be determined by suspending the model on its side and balancing it exactly horizontally. It is safest to have the imaginary extension of the tether passing through the model's C.G. in the vertical plane. The bridle attachment points must be firmly anchored to the internal structure, and the bridle is best made from piano wire or stranded cable, the ends being made off as in Fig. 195.

Rubber-driven Models

Rubber-driven models have the advantage of adjustable power—it is a simple matter to add or remove a loop or two of rubber. For high speed dashes two or more motors are used, driving the propeller through a gearbox (brass gears are adequate) as in Fig. 196. Even single-motor models are better for the incorporation of a gearbox, but chiefly in respect of duration of run (Fig. 197).

Many types of otherwise orthodox models can be rubber-driven by the system shown in Fig. 198. A tunnel is provided through the hull, with remov-

able plugs at each end. The stern plug carries the propeller and bearing, the bow plug the forward rubber anchorage and a winding loop. Flood-holes are provided so that the tunnel quickly fills when the boat is placed in the water. Large, fairly coarse pitch propellers are used for duration, small props with coarse pitch for speed.

A rubber motor should be made up by driving two pins in a clean board and winding the required number of strands round the pins. The total length of the finished motor should be about 20 per cent longer than the distance between the hooks. The ends of the strip should be tied off with a reef knot and the knot then stretched while a wool

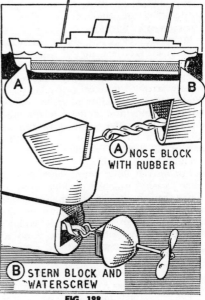

A NOSE BLOCK
WITH RUBBER

B STERN BLOCK AND
WATERSCREW

FIG. 198.

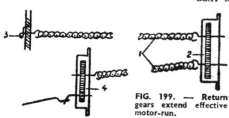

FIG. 199. — Return gears extend effective motor-run.

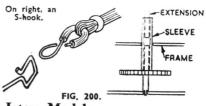

FIG. 200.

binding is put on each side; the ends are then trimmed off close. The loops at each end of the motor are bound tight with a rubber band. Before winding the motor should be lubricated, the best lubricant being a mixture of 49 per cent soft soap, 49 per cent glycerine, and 2 per cent sodium salicylate, simmered in an old tin for ten minutes. Castor oil can be used, however.

The motor must now be broken in by winding about half turns on and running off, then increasing the number of turns by about 10 per cent each time up to a full winding. For maximum turns, the motor must be stretched to about three times its original length and wound with a hand-drill. Fig. 199 shows the provision of an S-hook, padded with valve rubber, by which means the motor may be detached for winding.

Clockwork Models

Many old clocks and similar mechanisms yield excellent motors for model boat work. The escapement part can be discarded, and the spindle of one of the wheels extended by means of tubing soldered over ; its bearing must, of course, be drilled out to accommodate the tube diameter (Fig. 200). The drive can be taken from an extension of this tube, any of the lighter couplings previously detailed being suitable.

For heavier duty, gramophone motors offer easily-available motive power. Drive can be taken off the turntable spindle to a gearbox stepping up the propeller speed to a useful working figure. The governor can be removed

FIG. 201.

or employed as a speed control on the boat. A good quality motor will give a cruise lasting about ten minutes.

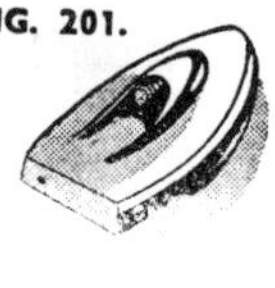

Jetex Models

Models powered by Jetex units are of necessity limited in their duration of run, although during the few seconds of power a well-designed model can cover 300 ft. or more. Structure is normally very lightweight, and balsa is the usual medium. Design follows that of hydroplanes, either single-step or three point suspension, the chief difference being in the above-water hull where, of course, provision has to be made for the efflux and motor access. Fig. 201 shows the usual lay-out.

Scale Sailing Models

Most scale sailing models need a slightly deeper-than-scale hull to give them adequate displacement for the somewhat over-scale structural weight and also to enable them to carry scale canvas. This latter may require some explanation, and, briefly, the reason is that when a yacht is scaled down, the righting moment of the lead keel is reduced to a greater extent than the heeling moment of the centre of effort (Fig. 202). For good sailing qualities, the lead must be increased, which means increasing the total weight of the model and thus its displacement. Deepening the hull achieves this without affecting the scale appearance of the

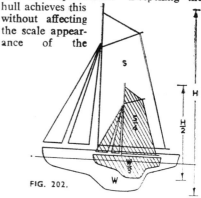

FIG. 202.

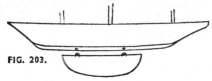

FIG. 203.

FIG. 204.

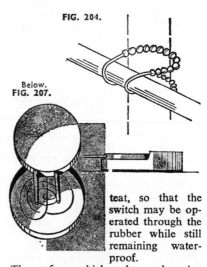

Below,
FIG. 207.

model when in the water.

A further difficulty encountered with any scale models, especially those with even one square sail (such as a topsail schooner) is that they will run and reach satisfactorily but are very poor to windward. Providing fin area helps this condition, and many builders adopt a detachable fin as in Fig. 203.

The difficulties of trimming an all square-rig model are usually overcome by securing the yards with rather free-fitting parrels (which can be simply lengths of copper wire threaded with tiny glass beads (Fig. 204), their vertical positions being ensured by the lifts. The yard braces are faked so that all yards are inter-connected, and one master-brace on each side will trim every one. Incidentally, the most frequent fault in scale sailing models is over-sparring and over-rigging. An air of delicacy is essential, and it far better to make spars and rigging too light than too heavy.

Submarines

Model submarines are particularly attractive, and lend themselves especially to rubber drive. If electric power is used, the access hatches must be screwed in place over a rubber seating, and a switch should be provided externally, over which is cemented a cut-off baby's

teat, so that the switch may be operated through the rubber while still remaining waterproof.

The surfaces which make a submarine dive are hydroplanes (Fig. 205), and these can be operated by a worm gear from inside, to produce a succession of diving and surfacing, or the planes can be spring-loaded to "dive" position and fitted with an arm (Fig. 206) on which is mounted a drag-plate (a scrap of celluloid) which can be adjusted in height or size to provide a submerged cruise or re-surfacing. Whatever system is used, if the model is made just positively buoyant, it will always surface at the end of the power run. A safety measure is a soldered-up tin, disguised as a gun mounting, equipped with a coil line, and stuck in place with soap (Fig. 207). If the model is stuck in weeds, or remains submerged for any other reason, the soap will slowly dissolve and allow the tin to surface.

By the way, to answer a common question, it is possible to radio-control a completely submerged model, but only if the model's aerial is completely insulated from contact with the water and fitted with a condenser.

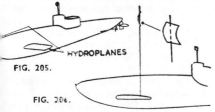

HYDROPLANES

FIG. 205.

FIG. 206.

Chapter Fourteen **Operation**

IT is a pity for romantics that a boat's first contact with the water usually comes some time before the last coat of paint is dry and the last detail fitted ; however, it is far more practical to test trim during construction, before alteration of the position of a component becomes a major operation. The time for this is after the initial two or three coats of paint and, if possible, before permanent attachment of the deck. Mark the waterline at stem and stern with pencil ticks, and place components, or equivalent weights, in correct positions, and check that the hull floats true. Very few models are larger than can be accommodated in the household bath, but if you have difficulty, many clubs have measuring tanks or, of course, the model can be checked in a pond.

If, after completion, ballast is required to bring the boat down to her marks, or to correct trim, determine the required amount and its position by stacking cut chunks of lead in place, then melt the lead into a convenient block and screw it in place in the hull as low as possible.

Prepare everything for the initial outing with care—tools, fuel or fresh batteries, rag, sponge, starting cord if necessary, spares, etc., and a pole and a sorbo ball with forty or fifty feet of twine attached. Establish a routine, since nothing is more frustrating than arriving at the water to find some essential item omitted. On arrival, check wind direction, current (if any), weed patches, and

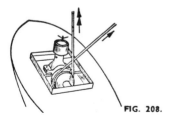

FIG. 208.

retrieving possibilities. A light, wide rake is often useful to clear small areas of surface weed.

Steam, electric, clockwork, or rubber power need no comment on starting procedure. I.c. engines need a starting cord, which may be a 3 ft. length of blind cord or $\frac{3}{16}$ in. leather belting or, best of all, a leather bootlace or similar thong. This is not wound round the flywheel groove (as with a full-size outboard), but merely passed beneath the flywheel, located in the groove, and crossed once (Fig. 208). The transom of the boat is gripped between the knees, and an assistant grips the bow (some men start single-handed by jamming the bow against a tree). The cord is gripped in both hands and the flywheel "rocked" backwards and forwards until the engine is firing. Light tension is then kept on the right-hand end and the left-hand pulled sharply away. If the motor doesn't start, the process is repeated.

Control over a diesel is obtained by adjustment of the contra-piston and needle-valve, and the running settings after starting, on land, are considerably different from the settings required when the boat is placed in the water, where the r.p.m. is much lower. The slower speed means later ignition, hence the contra-piston must be raised, and decreased carburettor draught means less fuel, hence the needle must be opened. These adjustments must be made as the boat is lowered in, or just beforehand— it depends on the individual engine and lay-out.

Spark ignition motors are controlled by an ignition advance and retard lever and a needle-valve, and although not so critical as diesels, some adjustment of these controls is usually necessary. Glow engines have only a needle control, but are quite touchy on this, and will need increased fuel as the revs. are slowed.

Rudder settings for cruising will vary with local conditions, but if a straight run is required it must be remembered that propeller torque will tend to crab the boat's stern, giving, normally, slight right turn. Once on its way, the model should be watched for incorrect trim—lifting or slamming of the bow, etc. Ballast should be added, or component positions altered to cure this.

A telescopic or sectionalised pole is often of great assistance where reeds or shallows exist, and for long range retrieving a sorbo ball, pierced and threaded with twine, which may be thrown over the model and drawn towards shore with every hope of entangling the model and recovering it, is most useful. The sponge in the kit is used for extracting unwanted water which may have found its way into the hull.

Any type of model should be thoroughly sponged down with clean fresh water after a day's sailing; the engine, etc., should be thoroughly cleaned and dried, tanks emptied, and, in fact, the whole boat left in a clean and "safe" condition.

Sailing Craft

It is most essential that a sailing model floats exactly on her designed waterline, otherwise she will never give her best performance. A table of weights is given with any reputable design, and this should be adhered to as closely as possible, any variation being adjusted by means of the amount of lead. A few ounces under the total required weight is a little advantage, since this means that trimming ballast may be incorporated.

After assembly at the pond-side, note the wind direction and walk to the downwind bank. Trim the main boom to swing about 20° off the centre-line and adjust the jib to make the same angle. The boat should now sail a beat, and will probably require to make two

FIG. 209.—A yacht on the starboard tack.

or more legs to reach the windward bank of the pond. Experiment with the sail trim to get the boat pointing as close to the wind as possible; only experience will enable you to get the best out of her, and you will know when she is trimmed too "tight" because she will come up into wind and remain "in irons", just being blown backwards. Ease off the main sheet slightly to prevent this. The expression "starboard tack", incidentally, means that the wind is blowing on the starboard or right-hand side of the boat (Fig. 209), and "port tack" is, of course, the reverse.

For running, the beating sheet is either unhooked from the horse or eased right out (depending on the steering gear), and the jib eased out to roughly 40°. Reaching calls for main and jib at 40°-45°—the exact settings depend on the individual yacht, and the type of steering gear fitted.

Sailing a yacht is an art, and one in which a minute of demonstration is worth ten written pages. The budding skipper can do no better than take his yacht along to one of the yacht clubs listed in Appendix III, or at least pay a visit to see other models being sailed. Even if there is no local club, have a day out and travel to the nearest, and don't be shy to introduce yourself and seek advice. Yachting enthusiasts are always delighted to meet a "convert", and will usually gladly give their time and experience in order to see him on the right path.

Chapter Fifteen

Radio Control

THE subject of radio control for model boats requires a whole book to itself, and it is therefore hoped that electronic wizards will be forbearing if only the basic outlines are described here. As on previous occasions in this book, it is necessary to consider power boats and sailing craft separately in the particular, although many of the comments made apply to either class in general. First, however, for the benefit of those who have yet to taste the joys of radio control, let us take a brief and non-technical look at the actual radio side.

Radio

Two frequencies are allocated by the G.P.O. for radio transmitters used for model work, and these are 26.96-27.28 megacycles, and 464-465 m/c. On the former the effective radiated power must not exceed 1.5 watts, and on the latter 0.5 watts. The 27 m/c band is used by 99 per cent of modellers in Great Britain so that remarks will be confined to this waveband. Readers should note that a licence is required to operate equipment; this is as simple as possible and entails no tests or anything of that nature. A licence costs £1.50 and covers five years, and is available from the Ministry of Posts and Telecommunications, Radio Regulatory Division, Waterloo Bridge House, Waterloo Road, London, S.E.1. Transmitting equipment can be purchased or constructed by individuals. Commercial transmitters are built and sealed to within the G.P.O. limitations, but if a home-built transmitter is to be used, it should first be checked against a signal generator, and the trimming condensers sealed with wax. The safest method is, of course, to use a crystal-controlled circuit, but constructional

details are beyond the scope of this short survey.

There are several systems of radio control calling for different types of equipment. The simplest is single-channel sequence control, where in effect the signal transmitted merely closes a switch at the receiver end. This entails the use of a sequence mechanism in the model, so that closing and opening the "switch" produces a set number of actions in strict order, and to repeat any action means that all the others have to be quickly gone through. The switch can be either a relay or a transistor switcher. A relay is an electro-mechanical device (Fig. 210) in which

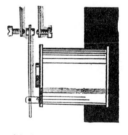

a blade moves across to close a contact when the current flowing in the receiver changes on receipt of a transmitted signal. An all-transistorised receiver simply changes its output current on receipt of a signal. In either case the result is to operate an escapement or actuator, the relay by completing a separate circuit including a battery, the transistor by its current change direct.

Normally, this action simply switches the escapement or actuator to operate the rudder, either left, neutral, right, neutral, or possibly left, right, neutral, but it is possible to operate a further control by what is usually termed a "blip" addition. This is operated by a quick signal from the transmitter, either by a very quick manual tap or an electronic blip, and this causes the actuator to "dwell" on a point of its rotation which it normally skips over. In dwelling, it switches on a second actuator which, typically, would operate a motor throttle or switch.

Pulse control, employing the relay blade to switch two circuits (Fig. 211), is a development of single channel control in which a continually pulsed signal

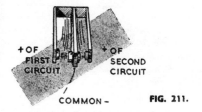

+ OF FIRST CIRCUIT

+ OF SECOND CIRCUIT

COMMON – **FIG. 211.**

is emitted by the transmitter and the actuators wired to the relay only operate when no signal or a full signal is sent. The transmitter pulsing can be electronic, electro-mechanical (e.g. a rotating drum, half conductive and half insulated, with wipers rubbing on it) or it can even be manually pulsed. This is an aspect of radio which was at one time popular with modellers who built their own radio and actuators, but is not now widely used, though some literature on the subject is still available for experimenters wishing to explore its possibilities.

More advanced radio, though now obsolescent, is multi-channel equipment in which the transmitter has superimposed upon its basic radio wave a series of oscillations or notes. These oscillations are passed through a reed bank or tone filters in the receiver, so that different frequencies are isolated to make individual "switches". Anything up to, normally, 12 selective controls can thus be chosen, with the appropriate response occuring to each. For a standard i.c. engined boat, only four channels or frequencies are needed, one each for rudder left and right and one each for throttle opening or closing. The transmitter would normally have only two keys, both sprung centrally, one moving

left or right for rudder and the other up and down for engine.

Reed systems are now regarded as second-rate for aircraft control, but are still entirely suitable for boats. This is because to apply, say, rudder for a wide turn, it is necessary to "tick" the key, which applies full rudder intermittently. The ratio between signal on and signal off determines the diameter of the turn, and it is a simple matter to learn to turn smooth circles of any diameter with a boat, since the relatively high viscosity of the water helps to damp out any jerkiness. With an aircraft, really smooth control is more difficult. Thus the swing away from reed or filter radio by aeromodellers meant a large number of outfits in excellent condition available second-hand, and many boat enthusiasts still use such equipment.

The advanced equipment now manufactured is of the "proportional" type, in which the controls in the model move exactly proportionally to the degree of movement of the transmitter controls. Thus, keeping to the same example, any degree of turn can be selected and held simply by moving the transmitter key the appropriate amount. To distinguish between sets, it is usual to refer to proportional equipment by its number of functions, and to achieve the equivalent of four-channel reed control, the proportional set would require two functions (i.e. rudder and engine).

How a proportional set works electronically is beyond the scope of this book, but the transmitter, receiver, and servos are all-transistorised and form a matched set, usually incorporating only one power source which can be dry batteries but is more frequently a sealed pack of nickel-cadmium cells which can be re-charged after every two or three hours of operation.

Actuators and Servos

A single-channel rudder-only control can use an escapement or actuator to operate the rudder; terminology gets a little loose at times, but an escapement is normally a device operated by a rubber or clockwork motor and the stored energy is allowed to "escape". Fig. 212 indicates a motor connected by a crank

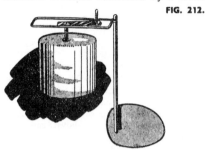

FIG. 212.

to the rudder tiller. The motor could be driven by current from the relay circuit or transistor switch when a signal is sent, but it would be a very hit-or-miss affair.

Fig. 213 shows the escapement principle; a rotor (driven by rubber or clock-

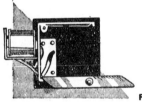

FIG. 213.

work) is engaged by an L-shaped pawl, and the pawl is rocked on receipt of a signal by means of a magnetic coil. As the retaining end is withdrawn, the rotor turns and comes up against the other end of the L, and when the signal ceases the L returns to its rest position under the influence of a light spring. The rotor then rotates a further 90 deg. A further signal repeats the operation and on

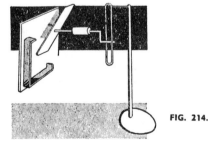

FIG. 214.

cessation the rotor has completed one revolution. Connected to a rudder as, for example, in Fig. 214, it will be seen that at either rest position the rudder will be central but that during a signal it will be held at full left or full right position. A four-armed pawl (Fig. 215) gives permanent rudder in the sense that one signal applies rudder and a

FIG. 215.

further signal moves the rotor on to the next neutral. A three-armed rotor pawl avoids the necessity of remembering the last rudder position since it can have only one neutral and therefore has a sequence from neutral of, say, one long signal for right rudder followed by a short second signal to return to neutral, or two signals, one short and the second long, for left, returning to neutral on release.

Rubber is not practical as a power source in a boat, compared with an aircraft, and clockwork escapements are in limited supply. Electric actuators overcome the problems of power supply and the necessity to re-wind; most are used in the same way as a three-armed escapement but instead of a pawl detaining the rotor, the stop positions are effected by electrical means, via a printed circuit disc and wipers.

Servos are mechanisms moving in either direction and requiring two reed channels (or one proportional function) to operate. They can be self-neutralising or progressive, i.e. left in any position. A servo used with proportional equipment moves according to the control position on the transmitter, and is (rather obviously) called a proportional servo. Model R/C servos are always electrically driven.

Most modern equipment is super-heterodyne and crystal controlled. This means that several sets can be operated simultaneously, the transmitters sending signals by differing frequencies, and identified by a colour code. Two equipments on the same frequency cannot operate together without interference. Some of the cheapest single-channel gear is super-regenerative, and only one such set can operate at a time.

Two final points which shold be mentioned. A cam on an actuator or servo can be used to close micro-switches or leaf contacts (Fig. 216) to control, say, an electric main propulsion motor or yacht's sail winch, and for slow "spectacular" models, when more operations are required, selector mechanisms can be used. There are several excellent ex-Government selectors available quite inexpensively, giving up to ten circuits. Any simple impulse motor can be arranged to drive a drum provided with contacts for more circuits than this if required. The basic system for a selector is a pawl pushing round a ratcheted wheel. The receiver relay closure energises a solenoid which attracts the pawl, pushing the wheel round one notch ; as the pawl moves, it breaks the solenoid circuit and a light spring returns it ready for the next impulse which, if the relay is still closed, occurs immediately the pawl re-makes the solenoid circuit. The wheel will thus click round until transmission ceases. Contacts may be spaced so that timing is not critical, but the usual system is to arrange them so that one transmission makes a contact, a second clears it, the third makes the next contact, and so on. Naturally, this calls for a feat of memory to select any particular

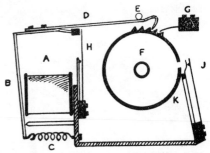

FIG. 217.—Principle of impulse motor. A—solenoid, B—armature, C—adjustable spring, D—spring arm, E—stop, F—toothed wheel, G—spring ratchet, H—solenoid contacts, J—contacts, K—spring. Contacts J are broken by notches in wheel, cutting solenoid current, which is switched on again by receiver relay.

operation, so the idea can be developed to produce an automatically timed transmission using a telephone dial, returning the selector to the same starting point after each operation.

Installation

The chief requirements for radio installation are space, access, and freedom from water. When a boat has reached the framing-up stage, the radio lay-out should be considered and appropriate holes for wiring, etc., fitted into the general construction. Normally the receiver is mounted forward of the engine bay and the steering gear fitted immediately in front of the transom ; batteries are stowed low, frequently under the receiver, but the fore-and-aft position of the boat's centre of gravity may affect their position.

All model power boats will suffer from some vibration, and yachts may be knocked from time to time, so the receiver and relay, in particular, must be mounted either on rubber seatings, or slung by means of rubber bands or springs (Fig. 218). The best method is to cut the centre out of a foam rubber bath sponge and mount the unit in the resulting "box", which may be glued or strapped in place. Standard practice in competition is to fit radio, etc., in a plastic sandwich box, which is waterproof, in a foam "bed".

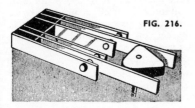

FIG. 216.

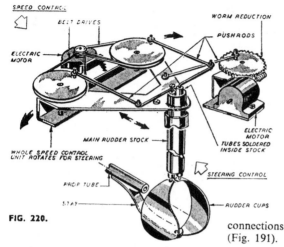

SPEED CONTROL

BELT DRIVES

ELECTRIC MOTOR

WORM REDUCTION

PUSHRODS

ELECTRIC MOTOR TUBES SOLDERED INSIDE STOCK

MAIN RUDDER STOCK

WHOLE SPEED CONTROL UNIT ROTATES FOR STEERING

STEERING CONTROL

PROP TUBE

STAY

RUDDER CUPS

FIG. 220.

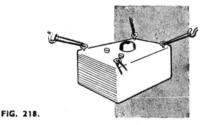

FIG. 218.

ously excluded from the radio parts. The engine compartment must be sealed off and the exhaust led out of the boat if you are using an i.c. motor; hatches should incorporate a water-seal (Fig. 68) to prevent stray splashes creeping in. It is also important to keep the batteries dry, and they, like every other part of the equipment, should be quickly removable, without the necessity of stripping half the boat! Radio batteries should be stowed in clips having permanently wired connections as for main motor batteries (Fig. 191).

A method of obtaining speed and steering control, including going astern without varying engine speed or direction is sketched in Fig. 220. This is known as a Kitchin rudder, and consists basically of two cups fitting round the propeller. The cups can be swung from side to side to provide steering, or progressively closed to produce backwash which will slow or stop the boat, or, when the cups pass a critical point, actually cause it to move astern. In the diagram, two circuits controllable by radio are required, one for steering and one for speed. Examination of the diagram will suggest other means of achieving the same control actions.

Neatness in wiring is essential; all joints must be sound and thoroughly soldered and unable to fracture from vibration (Fig. 219). Wires should be colour-coded, taped together and laid out in straight lines where possible, stapling to the structure. Keep wiring clear of the aerial, particularly that car-

WIRE

RUBBER SLEEVE

TAG.

FIG. 219.

rying H.T. Sockets must be kept clean, bright, and tight to ensure good contacts. Sloppy workmanship will keep you frustratingly on the bank, trying to trace an elusive fault, when you should be enjoying a pleasant, fully controlled cruise.

Dust, oil, exhaust fumes, and water—particularly salt water—must be rigor-

Yachts

R/C yachts appear at long last to be coming into their own. It is possible to sail a yacht with rudder control only but not very efficiently. It is also possible to have automatic sheeting worked by a vane switching gear, so that the yacht is simply set on the desired course by rudder application and the sails automatically set themselves.

Most people prefer to have full control of sheets and helm, and the commonest method is to have synchronous sheeting, i.e. both jib and main operate together and always maintain the same relative angle to each other. The sheets (usually attached to points on each boom an equal distance from the boom's pivot) are led to a winch drum, a lever type traveller (as described below) or sometimes to an endless belt or chain below deck.

Because of the advantage of sailing on some courses with slight helm, proportional equipment is desirable, but reeds (four channel) are quite suitable. A normal rudder servo can be used, but few sheeting mechanisms are commercially available as yet. Some skippers use a visual rudder indicator with a progressive servo (Fig. 221) and some prefer independent sheeting of jib and mainsail. Others use a spare pair of channels for rudder trim etc. Since the average boat uses a normal rudder servo, it is only necessary to outline one successful sheeting method.

FIG. 221.

FIG. 222.—A typical installation in which the sheets are first led through pulleys mounted on a samson post.

Both jib and main sheet are operated from a single traveller projecting above the deck (Fig. 222), which is driven in a cycle by a second motor. One function or two channels operate this. An alternative is a winch drum mounted on the motor, with gears, or an endless belt with the sheets attached at one point can be used. Another method is a long screwed rod with a jockey nut. A 6-8 second cycle is usual.

Naturally, the amount of sheet to be eased out to maintain the same relative settings of jib and main is smaller for the jib than for the main, due to the difference in the arc described by the clew of each sail; this is arranged by making the jib sheet off to a point nearer to the fulcrum of the traveller. The exact point can be determined by simple geometry, but in any event it is good idea to allow for one or two different hook positions as shown. The sheets are led through pulleys mounted on deck, either direct or via a post (Fig. 222).

One point which should not be underestimated is the power required to harden up the sheets—drawing in some five or six square feet of mainsail in a stiff breeze is no easy matter. Worm gearing is essential to drive the traveller operating crank, especially as with this type of gear backlash is avoided, and the sail force is not transmitted back to the motor, thus simplifying its starting.

The second method of control entails only the rudder mechanism operated by radio, so that reeds need not be used and pulse or a similar method of rudder selection may be employed.

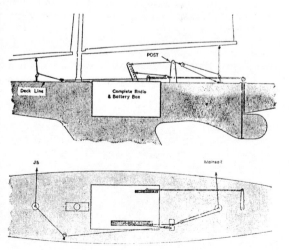

The sails are automatically set in accordance with the relative wind by means of a vane mounted in the usual place, but in this case merely serving to switch on the electric sheeting system. The switching is effected by the vane crank moving, through an arm, a contact set between two spring contacts. The contacts are mounted on a segment of gear driven off the sheeting mechanism, which is in the form of two drums (Fig. 223). Thus the vane will move round to adjust itself to a new wind direction when the yacht's course is changed by rudder application, and will re-trim the sails automatically. A moment's study of the diagram will make this system clear, and will no doubt start off a train of thought leading to other ways of doing the same thing.

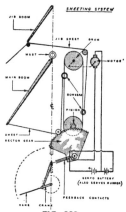

FIG. 223.

APPENDIX I

M.Y.A. RATING CLASSES

Model yachting in this country is controlled by the Model Yachting Association, and the following classes are current.

1. International A Class
This is the largest class and is the principle one used in International events. The rule to which it is built is rather complicated, but the basic formula is:
$(L + \sqrt{S} \div 4) + (L \times \sqrt{S} \div 12 \times 3 \sqrt{D}) = 39.37$,
where L is length, S sail area, and D displacement.

2. 10 Rater
The oldest rating class of all, and a rule which allows scope for experimentation to a large extent. The basis of the rule is the formula, $LWL \times SA \div 7,500 = 10$, where LWL is the load water line, and SA is the sail area.

3. 6 Metre IRYU Class
These are scaled down models of full-size craft to a rather complex rule formulated by the International Yacht Racing Union, and incorporating, bow, stern, and girth taxes, and other restrictions designed to produce a fairly standardised boat.

4. Marblehead Class
Marbleheads, or 50/800 designs, originated in the U.S.A., but are now extremely popular over here and in many other countries. The main features of the rule are that the length must not exceed 50 in., and the sail area must not exceed 800 sq. in.

5. 36 in. Restricted Class
This is perhaps the simplest rating rule of all, since it lays down only that the hull shall be capable of being contained in a box of inside dimensions 36 x 11 x 9. and the all-on weight of the model shall not exceed 12 lb.

Complete details of each of the above classes, sailing rules, etc., are available from the Hon. Publications Secretary, M.Y.A., V. E. Smeed, P.O. Box 35, Hemel Hempstead, Herts HP1 1EE, at modest cost (S.A.E. for price list). Interested builders may normally see copies at their nearest club, and are urged to approach the club first.

APPENDIX II

MM CLASS RATING RULES

L.O.A.: 25 in., ⅛ in. tolerance allowed.

Sail Area: Not to exceed 1½ sq. ft. (216 sq. in.).

Hull: Hollow garboard not less than ½ in. radius (can be checked with halfpenny).

Ballast: Movable ballast prohibited. Weight of ballast must not be altered during a race or series of races.

Bumper: (Or fenders) not included in L.O.A. but must not exceed ½ in. overhang.

Scantlings & Materials: No restriction.
No limit to L.W.L. beam, draught, freeboard, tumblehome, or displacement.

Prohibited: Movable keels, metal fin keels, or others without hollow garboard. Centre boards, lee boards, bilge boards, bowsprits, and overhanging rudders.

S.A. Measurement: Is taken as a simple triangle between head, tack, and clew; roach, bow, etc., are not measured.

Sail Battens: Jib or foresail—not exceeding 1 in. in length or three in number, dividing the leach into approximately equal parts. Mainsail—not exceeding 2 in. in length or four in number, dividing the leach into approximately four equal parts. No wire or other stiffening permitted in headsails.

Headboards: Shall not exceed ½ in. along the base.

Height of Rig: The jib shall not be attached to the mast at a height above the deck which exceeds 80 per cent of the height of the mainsail headboard above the deck.

Spinnakers: Are allowed; boom must not be more than 7½ in. in length, measured from the centre line of the mast to the outer end of the boom. Spinnaker must not be hoisted higher than point where jib stay cuts mast, hoist to be measured from where forestay cuts mast down to deck. Spinnaker headboard or stick not to exceed ½ in. across base. A spinnaker may not be set with a footyard or more than one sheet, nor any arrangement to spread the sail to other than a triangular shape. The sheet may be led round the luff of the forestay. Sleeves and tubular pockets not allowed.

Mast & Spars: No limit to height of mast. Material, weight, and section are not restricted and no additional measurements for area are required when other than a circular section is used. Hollow masts and spars are permitted, as are permanently bent ones and rotating or bipod masts. Masts and spars are not included in measurement of sail area. Measurements for sail are taken in exactly the same way for raking or vertical masts.

Alternate Rigs: Allowed provided S.A. does not exceed 216 sq. in.

Sheeting or Set of Sails: No contrivances or gadgets, e.g., outriggers may be used on head-sails or spinnaker. The spinnaker boom may not be taken forward to act as a bowsprit. A spinnaker may not be set without a boom. A jib or spinnaker may not be sheeted on to the main boom. Two mainsails may not be used at the same time.

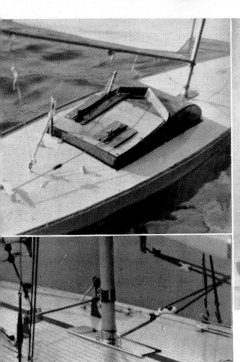

Top left, a radio controlled yacht, showing the travellers operating the tiller (starboard side) and sheets (port side), the latter via pulleys on a samson post. Above is "Water Baby", an example of the M.M. class yacht of which the chief rating features are overall length 25 in. maximum, and sail area 216 sq. in. maximum. Left, detail of a 10-rater showing jib horse and traveller, mast slide, kicking strap, chain plates and shrouds, and other fittings.

w is an advanced vane gear, which also incorporates some nts of the Braine system, and is fully graduated, so that any ment may be reset with accuracy. The pictures on the show a very simple gear which incorporates merely the principles of this ingenious method of steering; construc- the mechanism in the photographs is detailed in Chapter 8.

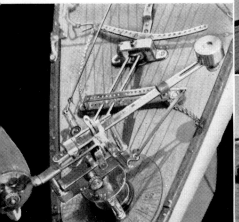

PLATE 7.

Left is "Foz II", one of the most suc
racing hydroplanes ever with a string of
three dozen first places to its credit
silencer does not cut down noise at close
but reduces the overtones which carry
Above is an example of double de
planking on a round bilge hull.

Above left, snapshots
as this of an anchor wi
as used on small tra
etc., can often be tak
holiday, and provide a
useful guide for later m
ling activities. Abov
popular choice of proto
is the motor torpedo
this example being the
9 in. "Thornycroft",
forms the prototype of
of the author's most po
commercial designs.
aerial views such as th
of "Pathfinder" e
authenticity in detai
proportions.

Below is an ultra-simple all balsa design featuring
box construction, in which structural rigidity is
achieved before planking by making the well of the
model part of the basic structure. The photograph on
the right is another holiday picture, showing the
stern part of a small trawler, and gives the prospective
builder some idea of the type of detail he may well
encounter! Noteworthy in this picture are the trawl
gallows.

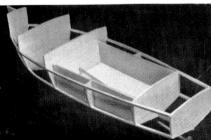

PLATE 8.

APPENDIX III

M.Y.A. AFFILIATED CLUBS

BARROW: E. R. Earles, 1a, Settle Street, Hibbert Road, Barrow-in-Furness.

BIRKENHEAD M.Y. & P.C.: W. Jones, 57, Forest Road, Birkenhead Cheshire.

BIRMINGHAM: D. Knowles, 104, Sharpe Street, Amington, Tamworth, Staffs.

BOURNVILLE M.Y. & P.B.C.: M. Harris, 1609, Stratford Road, Hall Green, Birmingham 28.

BURY: H. H. Salisbury, 314, Hornby Street, Bury, Lancs.

CLAPHAM: T. Knott, 23, Thirsk Road, S. Norwood, London S.E.25.

CLEETHORPES: G. Griffin, 13, Anderby Drive, Grimsby.

CORK: J. B. Horgan, 13, Denroche's Cross, Cork.

DANSON: G. W. Clark, 30, Carston Close, Lee, London SE12 8DZ. Tel. 01 690 6077.

EASTBOURNE & DISTRICT: C. E. Stacey, 22, Manor Way, Polegate, Sussex.

FALMOUTH & DISTRICT: E. G. Turvey, 28, Vernon Place, Falmouth.

FOREST GATE: F. J. Copper, 196, Handley Green, Swindon, Basildon, Essex.

FLEETWOOD M.Y. & P.B.C.: W. A. Rodrick, 18, Greenfields, Caton, Lancaster.

GOSPORT: W. E. Long, 2, Clovelly Road, Emsworth, Hants. Tel: Emsworth 2064

GUILDFORD: R. Stollery, 6, Little Tumners Court, Ballfield Road, Godalming, Surrey Tel: Godalming 21801.

HARWICH, DOVERCOURT & DISTRICT: D. Pratt, 5, Pepys Street, Harwich, Essex.

HIGHGATE: C. C. Marquis, 9, Carlton Gardens, Tufnell Park, London E.9.

HOVE & BRIGHTON: C. Colsell, 65, Ambersham Crescent, East Preston, Sussex. Tel: Rustington 71349.

LEEDS & BRADFORD: P. Maskell, 9, Andrew House, Town Street, Farsley, Pudsey, Yorks.

LONDON: J. Wheildon, 75, Breamwater Gardens, Ham, Richmond, Surrey.

MEDWAY MARINE MODEL SOCIETY: C. S. Gould, 40, Bredhurst Road, Wigmore, Gillingham, Kent.

M.Y.S.A.: A. E. Penney, 1, Paddock Heights, Twyford, Berks RG10 0AD.

NELSON GARDENS GREAT YARMOUTH: A. Burgess, 10 Laburnum Close, Bradwell, Great Yarmouth, Norfolk.

NEWCASTLE-ON-TYNE: G. Keeley, 70, Pilgrims Way, Durham Tel: Durham 63225.

NEW FOREST R/C M.Y.C.: R. C. Jefferies, 17, Colemere Gardens, Highcliffe-on-Sea, Hants. Tel: 4438.

NORFOLK & NORWICH: W. Grint, 12, Coppice Avenue, Hellesdon, Norwich.

NORTH LIVERPOOL: D. A. Clague, 9, Columbia Road, Walton, Liverpool.

NOTTINGHAM: L. Fowler, 2 Russell Avenue, Wollaton, Nottingham NG8 2BL.

PLYMOUTH: B. Boulden, 1, Lower Farm Road, New Park, Plympton, Plymouth, Devon.

POOLE: C. A. Sayer, 7, Shaftesbury Road, Poole, Dorset. Tel: Poole 2917.

PORTSMOUTH: M. Gowdy, 88, Folkestone Road, Copnor, Portsmouth.

RYDE: J. A. Buttigieg, 2, Gordon Road, Newport, Isle of Wight.

SCARBOROUGH: A. W. Sheppard, 22, Kingsway, Newby, Scarborough, Yorks.

SHEFFIELD: W. Tyler, 132, Handsworth Avenue, Sheffield 9.

SOUTHGATE: B. C. Wood, 90, Selbourne Road, Southgate, London N14 7DG.

SOUTH LONDON: W. Jupp, 83, Sussex Place, Slough, Bucks.

SOUTHAMPTON: W. Downie, 18, Eastbourne Avenue, Shirley, Southampton.

SOUTH SHIELDS: A. Vickers, 9 Elliott Gardens, South Shields.

TORBAY M.Y. & P.B.C.: D. Pinsent, 4, Barcombe Road, Paignton, Devon.
TYNEMOUTH: D. Greener, 55, Grange Road, Fenham, Newcastle-upon-Tyne.
WELWYN GARDEN CITY: J. K. Simpson, 3, Turpins Ride, The Chase, Welwyn, Herts.
WEST PENWITH: P. Lodey, 6, Kenstella Road, Newlyn, Penzance, Cornwall.
WICKSTEED: D. R. Warren, 158, King Street, Kettering, Northants.
Y.M.6m. O.A.: G. W. Clark, 30, Carston Close, Lee, London SE12 8DZ. Tel: 01 690 6077.

Hon. General Secretary M.Y.A.: R. Gardner, 6 Rowner Close, Rowner, Gosport, Hants.

(Please contact your nearest club rather than the M.Y.A. secretary, who is a voluntary official with limited time for replying to enquiries.)

APPENDIX IV

Power Boat Classification

There is as yet no world body for model power boats, the nearest being *Naviga,* which is an association of 15 countries and of which Britain is a member. The other 14 are Austria, Belgium, Bulgaria, Czechoslovakia, France, E. Germany, W. Germany, Holland, Hungary, Italy, Poland, Russia, Sweden, and Switzerland. Naviga classes are comprehensive, and include yachting, since a number of the member countries do not have national yachting associations and are not therefore members of the I.Y.R.U.

Classes are as follows:

A1—tethered hydroplanes, 0-2½ c.c.
A2—tethered hydroplanes, 2½-5 c.c.
A3—tethered hydroplanes, 5-10 c.c.
B1—tethered airscrew hydroplanes 0-2½ c.c. (radius of circle in all classes 15.923 metres, i.e., 100 m. circle, timing over 5 laps).
C—non-working models, 8 different categories.
D—free-sailing yachts, sailed in pairs over a course between 75 and 100 metres long, winner the first to pass between finishing buoys. Sub-divided into:
DF—International 10/40 class (l.o.a. 1 m., sail area 40 sq. dm.)
DM—Marbleheads.
D10—10-raters.
DX—unrestricted class, save that sail area must not exceed 50 sq. dm.
E—Straight runners, course as illustration, divided into:
EH—merchant or pleasure ships. EK—warships. EX—free-lance
F—radio classes, courses standard as sketches, sub divided into:
F1-E30—electric speed model with a maximum static power of 30 watts.
F1-E500—electric speed, power limited only to 42 volts.
F1-V2.5 i.c. engines 0-2½ c.c.
F1-V5—i.c. engines 2½-5 c.c.
F1-V15—i.c. engines 5-30 c.c.
F2—scale models, cloverleaf course, obligatory reverse, further split into:
F2a—length from 80 cm. to 110 cm. F2b—length from 110 cm. to 170 cm. F2c—length from 170 cm. to 250 cm. or 1/100th scale if larger.
F3—free-lance steering, Christmas tree course, divided into:
F3E—electric. F3V—i.c. engines.
F5—radio yachts, classes as under D. Triangular course of 150 m.
F6—Group manoeuvres (or team event) involving several boats. 7 mins. allowed.
F7—scale exhibition models capable of a number of functions. Time for demonstration 8 mins.
FSR—multi-boat racing, FSR 15 for all motors up to 15 c.c. and FSR 35 for spark ignition petrol engined models

It is of interest to note the records for Naviga classes, which of course constitute European records. At the time of printing, these are:

A1	J. Sustr	Czechoslovakia	155.575 k.p.h.
A2	K. Patsch	Russia	173.037 k.p.h.
A3	V. Subbotine	Russia	182.556 k.p.h.
B1	W. Marinco	Bulgaria	225.0 k.p.h.
F1-E30	A. Vohringer	W. Germany	45.7 secs.
F1-E500	C. Bordier	France	22.8 secs.
F1-V2.5	H. Gundert	W. Germany	19.0 secs.
F1-V5	A. Parapetti	Italy	18.3 secs.
F1-V15	K. Ripke	W. Germany	16.0 secs.

Records for F1 classes (R/C speed) are expressed as times to cover the standard course. There are no recognised world records since there is as yet no world standardisation on courses.

British Classes

In addition to the above classifications, the M.P.B.A. recognises four hydroplane classes, though two of these coincide with the Naviga classes. They are:

Class A—i.c. engines within a limit of 30 c.c., steam-driven boats restricted to an all-on weight of 16 lb.

Class B—i.c. engines within a limit of 15 c.c., steam-driven boats restricted to an all-on weight of 8 lb.

Class C—i.c. engines within a limit of 10 c.c., steam-driven boats restricted to an all-on weight of 5 lb.

Class D—i.c. engines within a limit of 5 c.c.

Straight-running boats are not restricted in any particular way (they correspond to EX class) except that they must not exceed 12 m.p.h. or use an engine larger than 35 c.c. General rules require engine silencing, drive by water-reaction, etc.

Radio boats have had a number of changes while this side of the hobby has been establishing itself; it is safe to make models to Naviga classes, however, since these fit into any rules which may foreseeably be adopted by the M.P.B.A. In fact the trend is towards standardisation on Naviga lines.

One type of R/C model rapidly growing in popularity is the "multi-racer", a rather loose term for a boat intended to race simultaneously against one or more other models, classified in Great Britain in three classes, 0–3½, 3½–6, and 6–35 c.c. The models are usually fairly robust—accidental collisions occur—and tend to follow the general shapes of offshore power boat racers. Model offshore power boat racing itself is in its infancy, but will become more popular.

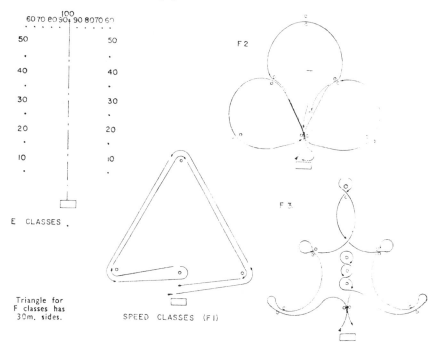

E CLASSES .

Triangle for F classes has 30m. sides.

SPEED CLASSES (F I)

F 2

F 3

APPENDIX V

Model Power Boat Association Affiliated Clubs

CLUB SECRETARIES (NORTHERN AREA)

ABERDEEN M.P.B.C.: A. Carnegie, 14 Marywell Caravan Site, Chickbar, Stonehaven Road, by Aberdeen.
ALTRINCHAM M.C. & B.C.: D. Innes, 122 Downham Crescent, Prestwich, Lancs.
BARNSLEY M.P.B.C.: G. Daniels, 250 Fresh Dam Lane, Carlton, Barnsley, Yorks.
BARROW S.M.S.: R. Newton, 86 Schneider Road, Barrow-in-Furness, Lancs.
BIRKENHEAD M.Y. & P.B.C.: A. Kanes, 21 Malvern Road, Wallasey, Cheshire.
BLACKBURN & DISTRICT: K. Howard, 20 Hornby Street, Oswaldtwistle, Lancs.
BRADFORD M.E.S.: G. S. Dunn, 13 Daisy Hill Lane, Bradford 9.
BRADFORD M.P.B.C.: J. Lindstrom, 87 Ashwell Road, Bradford.
BATLEY M.P.B.A.: B. Shaw, 59 Brookroyd Lane, Batley, Yorks.
BURNLEY M.P.B.C. (as Nelson).
CROSBY M.C.: W. Hayes, 4 Arnside, Litherland, Liverpool 21.
DONCASTER M.B.C.: J. D. Briggs, 10 Walden Avenue, Scawthorpe, Doncaster.
EDINBURGH P.B. GROUP.: G. F. Jorgenson, 32 Templerand Road, Edinburgh EH12 8RP.
FEATHERSTONE M.P.B.C.: Mrs. E. Brown, 11 Illingworth Avenue, Altofts, Normanton, Yorks.
FLEETWOOD M.Y. & P.B.C.: F. V. Benson, 10 Lymefield Grove, Stockport, Cheshire.
GLASGOW M.B.C.: G. Litchfield, 3 Faskally Avenue, Bishopbriggs, Glasgow.
HALIFAX M.B.S.: E. Peters, 18 College Terrace, Halifax Yorks.
HEATON & DISTRICT M.P.B.C.: T. E. Clement, 30 Cloverfield Avenue, Fawdon, Newcastle-on-Tyne NE3 3NL.
HUDDERSFIELD S.M.E.: C. Senior, 65 Spa Wood Top, Lockwood, Huddersfield, Yorks.
HULL M.C.: S. Barrett, 26 Inmans Road, Magdalen Lane, Hedan, Hull.
KEIGHLEY & DISTRICT M.E.S.: K. Parkin, 48 Park Road, Bingley, Yorks.
LEEDS M.B.S.: Mrs. P. Stott, 17 North Close, Roundhay, Leeds 8.
LIVERPOOL M.P.B.C.: J. Wilson, 53 Wandsworth Road, Liverpool L11 1OR.
MANCHESTER R.C.M.C.: F. Bradbury, 30 Green Park Rd, Northenden, Manchester 22.
MERCURY M.C.C.: J. B. Macfarquhar, 3 Kelbourne Street, Glasgow N.W.
NELSON & DISTRICT M.P.B.C.: N. Littler, 12 Dunderdale Avenue, Nelson, Lancs.
OSSETT & HORBURY M.M.S.: L. Barton, 3 Stevenson Drive, Barugh Green, Barnsley, Yorks.
OLDHAM M.C.: R. Lees, 8 Carbrook Crest, Carbrook, Stalybridge, Ches.
OLDHAM & WEST PENNINE M.B.R.C.: E. Wells, 31 Princess Street, Glossop, Derbyshire.
SCARBOROUGH M.Y. & B.C.: D. Newsome, 8 Dean Road, Scarborough, Yorks.
SHEFFIELD S.M.S.: C. R. Edwards, 100 Lupton Road, Sheffield S8 7NG.
S. SHIELDS M.Y.C.: A. B. Vickers, 9 Elliot Gardens, S. Shields, Co. Durham.
SPENBOROUGH M.E.S.: A. C. Keeling, Grange Nurseries, Westgate Hill, Bradford, Yorks.

SUNDERLAND M.E.S.: W. S. Wilson, 1 Overdene, Dalton-le-Dale, Seaham, Co. Durham.
TYNEMOUTH M.B.C.: S. Davidson, 21 Athol Gardens, West Monkseaton, Whitley Bay, Northumberland.
WIGAN M.P.B.C.: B. Heyes, 120 Wigan Lower Road, Standish Lower Ground, Wigan, Lancs.
WIRRAL RACING.: G. Nixon, 20 Leasowe Road, Wallasey, Cheshire.

CLUB SECRETARIES (MIDLAND AREA)

BARRY M.C.: (Tres.) B. O'Donovan, 29 Heol Ffynnan Wen, Whitchurch, Cardiff.
BIRMINGHAM S.M.E.: A. Reason, 23 Ashfurlong Crescent, Sutton Coldfield, Wk.
BOURNVILLE M.P.B.A.: K. Daniels, 71 Adams Hill, Bartley Green, Birmingham 32.
BLOXWICH M.P.B.C.: B. J. Chapman, 25 Tintern Crescent, Bloxwich, Staffs.
CLEETHORPES M.B.C.: G. Griffin, 13 Anderley Drive. Grimsby, Lincs.
COTSWOLD M.M.C.: R. J. Hill, 7 Berkeley Close, Cashes Green, Stroud, Glos.
COVENTRY M.E.S.: K. Medcalfe, 294 Allesley Old Road, Coventry.
CAERPHILLY M. & R.C.C.: J. H. Skinner, 27 Station Terrace, Caerphilly, Glam.
COVENTRY (RADIO CONTROL): A. Bird, 87 Sedgmoor Road, Coventry.
GWENT M.P.B.C.: K. M. Harris, 82 Laurel Road, Bassaleg, Mon.
LEICESTER: T. C. Lister, 149 Landsdowne Grove, South Wigston, Leicester.
LINCOLNSHIRE: L. R. Belton, 3 Gregg Hall Close, Lincoln.
MALVERN & DISTRICT M.P.B.A.: Miss M. Garbutt, Glen Lyon, Storridge, Malvern, Worcs.
NORTH BIRMINGHAM M.P.B.C.: F. Goff, 15 Plaistow Avenue, Birmingham B36 8HG.
NORTH WALES M.A.: S. Rodwell, 9 St. Davids Road, Llandudno, N. Wales.
NOTTINGHAM M.Y. & P.B.C.: M. Brentnall, 39 Denman Gardens, Ilkeston Road, Nottingham.
PORT TALBOT: N. B. Morris, 17 Eagle Street, Port Talbot, Glam.
RICHARD, THOMAS & BALDWIN (SPORTS & SOCIAL): F. Probert, 20 Heathfield Close, Garnlydan, Ebbw Vale, Mon.
ROLLS ROYCE (WELFARE): B. J. Minton, 14 Chesterfield Avenue, Long Eaton, Notts.
SHREWSBURY: A. R. Arbon, 30 Preston Grove, Trench, Telford, Salop.
WALSALL M.P.B.C.: J. G. Grainger, 108 Caldmore Road, Walsall, Staffs.
WICKSTEED M.Y. & P.B.C.: D. R. Warren, 158 King Street, Kettering, Northants.
WULFRUNA M.P.B.C.: J. E. Golding, 2 Vauxhall Gardens, New Rowley Road, Dudley, Worcs.

CLUB SECRETARIES (SOUTHERN AREA)

ANDOVER & DISTRICT M.P.B.C.: D. Swatton, 6 Leigh Gardens, Andover, Hants.
BASILDON M.P.B.C.: K. Norfor, 21 Codenham Green, Basildon, Essex.
BEXLEY & DISTRICT M.P.B.C.: J. Stocking, 99 Brightside Road, London S.E.13.
BLACKHEATH M.P.B.C.: D. Palfrey, 41 Ennersdale Road, Lewisham, S.E.15.
BRENTWOOD M.B.C.: J. A. Wentworth, 5 St. Charles Road, Brentwood, Essex.
BRIGHTON & HOVE S.M.E.: E. J. Meeds, 116 Islingwood Road, Brighton 7.
BRISTOL S.M.E.E.: A. Cooke, 32 Abbots Road, Hanham Green, Bristol BS15 3NG.
BROMLEY M.P.B.C.: G. O. Caird, 26 Blackbrook Lane, Bickley, Kent.
BUCKANEERS M.C.: D. Giles, "Derrons", Station Road, Bow Brickhill, Bletchley, Bucks.
CAMBRIDGE M.B.C.: J. R. Haynes, 14 Granta Road, Sawston, Cambridge.
CANVEY ISLAND M.A.: A. Bedingham, 46 Monks Haven, Stanford-le-Hope, Essex.
CLAPHAM M.P.B.C.: J. R. Donegan, 27 Whittaker Court, Clapham Road, London S.W.4

CYGNETS, MAIDSTONE: J. L. Cundell, 12 Hillshaw Crescent, Strood, Kent.
DOVER M.P.B.C.: D. R. Nelson, 36 Sandwich Road, Whitfield, Dover, Kent.
EASTBOURNE M.P.B.C.: B. J. Kemp, 9 Windmill Road, Polegate, Sussex.
FOLKESTONE M.C.: D. Powis, 38 Ashley Avenue, Cheriton, Folkestone.
HAMPSHIRE & S.C. M.H.C.: J. Hampton, 71 Winter Road, Southsea, Hants.
HANWELL & DISTRICT M.C.: P. South, 420 Greenford Avenue, Hanwell W.7.
HARROW & WEMBLEY S.M.E.: P. N. Reed, 5 Rydal Gardens, N.W.9.
HASTINGS M.P.B.C.: B. R. Saint, 38B Chiltern Drive, Hastings, Sussex.
HATFIELD & DISTRICT S.M.E.: F. W. Dunham, 57 Lockleys Crescent, Hatfield, Herts.
HEMEL HEMPSTEAD M.B.C.: C. W. East, 51 Micklem Drive, Hemel Hempstead, Herts.
HERTFORD: D. J. Metcalf, 3 Broadmeads, off Amwell End, Ware, Herts.
HIGHGATE M.P.B.C.: J. H. Bates, 70 Constantine Road, N.W.3.
KINGFISHER M.P.B.C.: D. R. Hill, 46 Somerset Road, Farnborough, Hants.
KINGSMERE M.P.B.C.: B. Nunn, 23 Joubert Street, London S.W.11.
MAYSBROOK M.P.B.C.: R. Hunter, 13 Boleyn Gardens, Dagenham, Kent.
MEDWAY M.M.S.: P. Richman, 110 St. Johns Road, Gillingham, Kent.
MID-ESSEX M.P.B.C.: D. R. Harvey, 116 Rickstones Road, Witham, Essex.
MORTLAKE & DISTRICT M.E.S.: P. Clisby, Flat 8, Block M, Peabody Estate, London, W.6.
NEW CITY M.S.: H. Severne, 4 Buckingham Street, Wolverton, Bucks.
NORTH LONDON S.M.E.: R. G. Clark, 114 Croftdown Road, London, N.W.5.
PORTSMOUTH & DISTRICT M.P.B.C.: F. Body, 18 Baileys Road, Southsea, PO5 1EA.
ST. ALBANS M.E.S.: P. Lambert, 6 Molescroft, Farm Avenue, Harpenden, Herts.
SOUTHAMPTON M.P.B.C.: L. Daish, 7 Bracken Lane, Shirley, Southampton.
SOUTHEND M.P.B.C.: R. Cockman, 29 Kensington Road, Southend-on-Sea, Essex.
SOUTH LONDON M.P.B.C.: C. F. Robe, 32A Sydenham Park Road, London, S.E.26.
STEVENAGE M.A. & M.S.: D. Walton, 39 Chertsey Rise, Stevenage, Herts.
ST. AUSTELL & DISTRICT M.C.: G. Payne, 85 Agar Road, St. Austell, Cornwall.
SWINDON M.P.C.B. & E.C.: R. Crawford, 22 Harcourt Road, Swindon, Wilts.
TORBAY R.C.M.B.C.: E. L. Dixon, "Higher Dunstone", Ashprington, Totnes, Devon.
VACUMATIC M.P.B.C.: Mrs. J. Rogers, 194 Harwich Road, Little Clacton, Essex.
VICTORIA M.S.C.: N. G. Phelps, 17 Jersey Road, Leytonstone, London, E.11.
WALTHAMSTOW M.C.: D. J. Harvey, 7 Strafford Avenue, Clayhill, Ilford, Essex.
WARE R.C.S.: E. J. Caunt, 164 Tower Road, Ware, Herts.
WATFORD M.M.C.: G. G. Nicholls, 63 Cassiobury Drive, Watford, Herts.
WELWYN G. C. S.M.E.: J. K. Simpson, 3 Turpins Ride, Welwyn, Herts.
WEST LONDON M.P.B.C.: A. Perman, 96 Kynaston Avenue, Thornton Heath, Surrey.
WOOD GREEN & DISTRIC M.P.B.C.: A. F. Miles, 5 Courcy Road, London, N.8.

Hon. Sec. M.P.B.A.: G. Colbeck, 19 Lea Walk, Harpenden, Herts.

(Please contact your nearest club rather than the M.P.B.A. secretary, who is a voluntary official with limited time for replying to enquiries.)

APPENDIX VI—BRITISH i.c. ENGINES

BRITISH I.C. ENGINES CURRENTLY PRODUCED OR IN POPULAR USE

ENGINE	DISPLACEMENT c.c.	DISPLACEMENT cu. in.	CYLINDER bore	CYLINDER stroke	WEIGHT* (oz.)	WORKING R.P.M.	MOUNTING	INDUCTION	FLYWHEEL Wt. oz.	FLYWHEEL diam.	FLYWHEEL thickness	PROPELLER diam.	PROPELLER pitch
D.C. Dart	.55	.036	.35	.35	1.25	9–14,000	R or B 1 1/16	FR	1 3/4	1 1/8	7/16	1 1/4	1 3/4
D.C. Merlin	.76	.047	.375	.420	1.75	9–14,000	R or B 1 3/16	FR	2	1 3/16	7/16	1 1/2	2
M.E. Heron	.97	.06	.424	.420	2.4	7–10,000	B 7/8	FR	3 1/2	1 1/4	5/8	1 1/4	1 1/2
D.C. Spitfire	.97	.059	.425	.42	6.7 inc.	8–14,000	R or B .82	FR	2.6	1.2	1/2	1 1/4	1 1/2
E.D. Fury	1.5	.090	.5	.468	3.625	8–14,000	B 7/8	RR	3 1/4	1 3/8	5/8	1 1/2	2
Frog 150	1.49	.091	.5	.46	3.25	11–14,000	R or B 7/8	FR	3 1/4	1 3/8	5/8	1 1/2	2
M.E. Snipe	1.48	.09	.505	.455	4.1	9–14,000	B 13/16	FR	4 3/4	1 1/4	3/4	1 1/4	2
D.C. Sabre	1.49	.091	.525	.42	3.0	10–12,000	B 7/8	FR	3 1/4	1 3/8	5/8	1 1/2	2
E.D. Racer	2.46	.15	.59	.55	5.4	10–15,000	B 1 1/8	RD	6	1 5/8	1/2	1 3/4	3
Frog 2.49	2.49	.151	.580	.568	6.0	10–13,000	B 1 1/16	FR	6	1 3/4	3/4	1 1/2	2 1/2
E.D. Sea Otter	3.46	.211	.656	.625	10.5	3–12,000	B 1 1/4	RD	7	2	1/2	1 3/4	2
Frog 3.49	3.47	.208	.666	.600	6.7	5–12,000	B 1 1/8	RD	7 1/2	1 1/2	1	1 1/2	2 1/2
E.D. Hunter	3.46	.211	.656	.625	16.5 inc.	3–12,000	B 1 1/4	RD	7	1 1/2	1 1/2	1 3/4	2 1/4
Oliver Tiger Major	3.47	.212	.620	.705	6.0	8–14,000	B 1 1/8	FR	5	1 3/8	3/4	1 3/4	3
E.D. Viking	4.9	.29	.78	.625	19.5 inc.	4–12,000	B 1 1/4	RD	6.4	1.6	1	2	2 1/2
Miles 5	4.92	.30	.781	.625	12.0	5–13,000	B 1 1/4	RD	7 1/4	2	5/8	2	3
Eta 29	4.95	.30	.750	.672	6.5	4–15,000	B 1 1/4	RD	4 1/2	1 5/16	1	2	3
Merco .49	8.0	.49	.880	.805	12.5	3–12,000	B 1 1/4	FR	12	1 3/4	1 1/8	2 1/2	3
Taplin Twin Mk II	8.0	.488	(2).705	.625	17.5	2– 9,000	B 1 1/4	SP	10 1/2	1 7/8	1	2 1/2	2 1/2
Merco 61	10.0	.61	.938	.875	13.0	3–12,000	B 1 1/2	FR	12	1 3/4	1 1/8	2 1/2	4
Miles 10								RD					
Taplin 15cc Twin	15.0	.9	(2).827	.846	32.0	2–12,000	B 1 9/16	RD	22	2	1	2 1/2	4
Gannet 15 Glow								FR					
Gannet O.H.V.	14.98	.92	1.06	1.03	28.0	1–10,000	B 2	4 str.	16	3	1/2	2 3/4	3
Miles 15								RD					

*Weights are normally without flywheel and w/c head.
R Radial, B Beam; dimensions with B are crankcase clearance in inches, i.e. distance between bearers for mounting
FR Front Rotary, SP Sideport, RD Rotary Disc or drum (rear).
Flywheels vary in weight depending on degree of counter boring. Weights given are either as supplied by makers or recommeded minimum.
Propeller sizes are suggested from experience, but will vary according to hull shape and weight, blade shape and number, efficiency, etc. Engines for which no figures are given are in limited production and have not been submitted for test.

APPENDIX VII — BRITISH ELECTRIC MOTORS

NAME	TYPE	WEIGHT & SIZE	OPERATING VOLTS	SHAFT & BEARINGS	BRUSHES	STALL TEST Current Torque (Amps)(oz.-in.)	FREE RUNNING Current (Amps) R.P.M.	TYPICAL PERFORMANCE FIGURES	REMARKS & 'MODEL MAKER' ISSUE IN WHICH REVIEWED
Ever Ready TG18, TG18B, TG18E	Perm. Magnet D.C	1¼ oz. 1 in. dia. 1 $\frac{3}{32}$ in. long	3 min. 6 max.	$\frac{1}{16}$ in. dia. Bronze: Self-lubricating	—	2.2 1.0 6 volts	0.2 8,000 6 volts	.15 amps at 7,000 .25 " " 11,000 .5 " " 6,000 .8 " " 9,000 At 6 volts *	Plastic Case, available without mount (TG18), or end mount (TG18E) or base mount (TG18B) (October, 1955)
Mighty Midget	Perm. Magnet D.C.	1⅝ oz. L.O.A.: 1⅝ in. Height: 1⅛ in.	3 min. 6 max.	$\frac{1}{16}$ in. dia. Self-lubricating	Flat Strip	0.8 0.3-0.4 6 volts	0.17 11,200 6 volts	.29 amps at 8,500 .37 " " 7,500 .52 " " 5,800 At 6 volts †	Reduction Gear (6:1) with countershaft and pulley. Black plastic case (August, 1955)
Taplin	Perm. Magnet D.C.	1½, 1 in. dia.	4.5	$\frac{1}{16}$ in. dia. Plastic	Copper Carbon	1.0 3.7 (gear shaft) 6 volts	0.13 8,400 6 volts	2 oz./in. at 350-500 r.p.m. (gear shaft)	Integral gears, 11.76:1 reduction (November, 1955)
Frog Tornado	Perm. Magnet D.C 3-pole	1¼ oz L.O.A. 1⅝ in. dia. 1 in.	3 min. 4.5 max.	$\frac{1}{16}$ in. dia. Plastic Drive Pin Brass	Flat Strip	1.3 0.5 4 volts	0.15 8,600	5,500—8,000 r.p.m.*	Alnico Field Magnet. Moulded Plastic case (May, 1955)
Frog Revmaster	Perm. Magnet D.C 3-pole	3¼ oz. 2 in. long × 1½ in × 1⅛ in.	4.5 min. 8 max.	⅛ in. dia. Brass	Copper Carbon Self-compensating	1.2 0.75-1.0 6 volts	0.2 5,600 6 volts	3,500—6,000 r.p.m.*	All-metal construction. Plastic brush holders. Metal pulley and drive pin assembly
Frog Whirlwind	Perm. Magnet D.C 3-pole	3¼ oz. 1½ in. dia. 2 in. long	4.5 min. 8 max.	⅛ in. dia. Bronze: Self-lubricating	Copper Carbon Self-compensating	1.2 0.7-0.8 6 volts	0.2 5,800 6 volts	4,400—6,600 r.p.m.*	Alnico Field Magnet. Red plastic case. Metal pulley and drive pin assembly
Bassett-Lowke 1461	Perm. Magnet D.C. 3-pole	5⅝ oz. Length: 2½ in. × 2 in. × 1¼ in.	4.5 min. 6 max.	$\frac{3}{32}$ in. dia. Brass	Flat Strip	1.7 1.0-1.25 6 volts	0.4 3,650 6 volts	R.p.m. on load 2,000—2,500* 4.5—6 volts	All-metal construction Cobalt steel Field Magnet
Taycol Comet	Perm. Magnet D.C. 3-pole	5¾ oz. Base: 2 in. × 1⅝ in. Height: 2¼ in.	4.5 min. 6 max.	$\frac{3}{32}$ in. dia. Paxolin	Flat Strip	2.4 1.0-1.75 6 volts	0.56 5,200 6 volts	4,500—6,000 r.p.m.*	Upright construction. Paxolin end plates (September, 1955)
Taycol Star	Perm. Magnet D.C. 3-pole	5¼ oz. Base: 3⅜ in. × 2¼ in. Height: 1⅝ in.	4.5 min. 9 max.	$\frac{3}{32}$ in. dia. Brass Trunnion	Flat Strip	5.0 1.0 6 volts	0.7 7,400 (max.)	—	Fitted with speed control and reversing switch
Taycol Geared Comet	Perm. Magnet D.C. 3-pole	6¼ oz. Base: 2⅜ in. × 1⅝ in. Height: 2¼ in.	4.5 min. 6 max.	$\frac{3}{32}$ in. dia. Paxolin Brass Gears	Flat-Strip	2.4 4.0-5.0 6 volts	0.55 1,350 (drive shaft) 6 volts	1,200—1,500 r.p.m.*	4:1 Reduction Gear to drive Shaft (September, 1955)

NAME	TYPE	WEIGHT & SIZE	OPERATING VOLTS	SHAFT & BEARINGS	BRUSHES	STALL TEST Current (Amps) Torque (oz.-in.)	FREE RUNNING Current (Amps) R.P.M.	TYPICAL PERFORMANCE FIGURES	REMARKS & 'MODEL MAKER' ISSUE IN WHICH REVIEWED
Taycol Twin-Geared Comet	Perm. Magnet D.C. 3-pole	$6\frac{3}{4}$ oz. Base: $2\frac{3}{8}$ in. x $1\frac{5}{8}$ in. Height: $2\frac{1}{4}$ in.	4.5 min. 6 max.	$\frac{3}{32}$ in. dia. Paxolin Brass Gears	Flat-Strip	2.4 Not De-terminable 6 volts	0.6 1,150 (drive shafts) 6 volts	1,500 r.p.m.*	4:1 Reduction Gear to drive Shafts. Two Drive Shafts (contra-rotating) (September, 1955)
Taycol Torpedo	Perm. Magnet D.C. 3-pole	$12\frac{1}{2}$ oz. Base: $2\frac{1}{4}$ in. x $1\frac{5}{8}$ in. Height: $2\frac{3}{4}$ in.	6	Paxolin	Dimpled Phos. Bronze	1.3 3 6 volts	— 6,500	3,300 r.p.m. on 2 v. 7,850 r.p.m. on 12 v.	2-12 v. supply (December, 1955)
Bassett-Lowke Marine (1466)	Perm. Magnet D.C. 3-pole	$11\frac{1}{2}$ oz. Base: $3\frac{1}{4}$ in. x 2 in. Height: $1\frac{3}{4}$ in.	6 min. 8 max.	$\frac{3}{32}$ in. dia. Brass	Copper Carbon Self-compensating	3.6 6.25 8 volts	0.44 3,800 8 volts	2,500—3,000 r.p.m. on load* 6—8 volts	All-metal construction. Dural Base, Pulley and Drive Pin Assy. Std.
Gov. Surplus C.M.3 —	Split coil D.C. 9-pole	11 oz. Length: $2\frac{7}{8}$ in. x $1\frac{5}{8}$ x $1\frac{5}{8}$	12	$\frac{5}{32}$ in. dia.	Self-compensating	1.9 4.5 12.5 volts	.6 4,800 12.5 volts	—	Irreversible (March, 1955)
Gov. Surplus 5U/4798 Sallis	Perm. Magnet D.C. Multi-Pole	$4\frac{1}{2}$ oz. $1\frac{1}{4}$ in. dia. 2 in. long	12 min. 24 max.	.120 in. dia. Self-lubricating	—	0.64 2-2.75 11.9 volts	0.13 3,400 11.9 volts	—	Very smooth. Vibrationless running
5U/2705 Sallis	D.C. Multi-Pole	$1\frac{3}{4}$ lb. $3\frac{1}{4}$ in. x 2 in. x 2 in.	24	$\frac{1}{8}$ in. dia —	—	3.5 12.5 11.8 volts	0.65 3,400 11.8 volts	—	Operates well on 12 volt supply (July, 1955)
Meccano E020	Universal (A.C.-D.C.) 3-pole	$12\frac{1}{2}$ oz. $2\frac{1}{2}$ in. dia. 2 in. long	20 min. 25 max.	$\frac{1}{8}$ in. dia. Plain-oil lubricated	Carbon sprung loaded	— — Not Determined	— 4,000* Not Determined	6 oz.-in. at 2,000 r.p.m.* (20 volts, 50 cps. supply)	Die-cast casing. Black crackle finish
Bassett-Lowke Super Marine	Perm. Magnet D.C. 3-pole	1 lb. 15 oz. Base: $4\frac{1}{2}$ in. x $2\frac{1}{2}$ in. Height: $1\frac{1}{2}$ in.	6 min. 8 max.	$\frac{3}{16}$ in. dia. Brass	Copper-Carbon Spring loaded	9.5 15.0 11.8 volts	0.6 6,000 11.8 volts	2,000—2,500 r.p.m. on load*	Cobalt Steel Field Magnet (January, 1955)
Mersey Marine Navigator	Shunt D.C. 8-pole	20 oz. Length: 5 in. x 3 in. x 2 in.	12	Steel $\frac{3}{16}$ in. Bronze	Self-compensating	— 12.5 12 volts	— 5,600* 12 volts	850—1,000 on load. 1.5 amps.	Integral gearbox (three shafts). Suppressed (April, 1955)
Meccano E20R	Universal (A.C.-D.C.) 3-pole	16 oz. Base: $3\frac{1}{2}$ in. x $2\frac{1}{2}$ in. Height: $2\frac{1}{2}$ in.	20 min. 25 max.	$\frac{5}{32}$ in. dia. Brass	Copper-Carbon Spring loaded	Not Determined	— 7,500* Not Determined	10.5 oz.-in. at 1,900 r.p.m.*	Open Frame (Metal) Double Shaft Extension fitted 19-tooth Pinion, $\frac{1}{2}$ in. dia. Fitted Reversing Switch (February, 1955)
Taycol Marine	Split Field D.C.	38 oz. $3\frac{1}{2}$ x $3\frac{1}{2}$ x $2\frac{1}{2}$	6	$\frac{1}{4}$ in. dia. Paxolin lubricated	Copper mesh	6.4 35 6 volts	1.05 4,800 6 volts	2.55 amps at 1,500 2.1 amps at 2,000	May be used for direct drive (June, 1955)

*Manufacturer's Figures. †N.P.L. Figures.

Glossary

Some of the more common nautical terms, full-size and model.

ACTUATOR.—A mechanism for moving controls, etc., set into action by means of radio.

AFT (Abaft, After).—Towards the stern or rear.

AIRSCOOP.—A simple type of ventilator for small craft.

ALOFT.—Above deck.

AMIDSHIP ('midship).—Central.

ANODE CURRENT.—An electrical current permanently flowing when a valve is in operation, changed by receipt of radio signal.

ATHWARTSHIP.—In the lateral plane.

AUDIO TONE.—A means of radio control using differing frequencies imposed on a carrier wave.

BACK-LASH.—Taking up of play in gears by back pressure.

BACKSTAY.—Line leading down from the mast to brace it from aft.

BAFFLE.—A perforated plate set in the fuel tank, etc., to reduce liquid surge.

BALLAST.—Extra weight usually in the form of lead added to bring a boat to its correct water-line.

BALLOON JIB.—A very large headsail, sometimes used on a racing yacht.

BANG-BANG RUDDER.—In radio control a rudder which has only three positions, full left, neutral, or full right.

BARBETTE.—Circular mounting for gun turret or other rotating fitting.

BARQUE.—A three masted vessel square-rigged on fore and main, and fore and aft rigged on mizzen.

BARQUENTINE.—A three masted vessel square-rigged on foremast, fore and aft rigged on main and mizzen.

BEAM.—The greatest width of a boat, also one of the timbers on which the deck is laid.

BEATING SHEET.—A line controlling the angle to which the main boom of a yacht may swing.

BELAY.—To make fast a rope, to stop.

BELAYING PIN.—A brass or wooden pin set in a pin rail for securing running rigging.

BEND.—To fasten in place.

BILGE.—The portion of the hull below water, also the inside of the hull where extraneous water collects.

BINNACLE.—A container for a ship's compass.

BLOCK.—A pulley which is used in rigging.

BLUSHING.—Whitening of cellulose liquids due to chemical reaction with water vapour on drying.

BOAT.—Formerly a vessel built on bent frames (a ship used sawn frames), but nowadays any vessel which is capable of being hoisted aboard another vessel ; except in the R.N., generally applied to any vessel at all.

BOAT CHOCKS.—Wood cradles for stowing a boat.

BOLLARD.—Sturdy posts normally set in pairs for making off cables, etc.

BOLT ROPE.—A rope sewed to the edge of a sail for strengthening.

BOOM.—A spar at the foot of the sail.

BOOT TOP.—A painted line or changing colour at the hull water line.

BOW.—The forward part of a vessel.

BOWSIE (Bowser).—A small slide used in a model's rigging.

BOWSPRIT.—A spar projecting forward of the bow from which headsails are set.

BRACE.—A line leading up from the yard arms to control the yard position horizontally.

BRAIL.—The rope used to assist the furling of a fore and aft sail.

BREAD AND BUTTER.—Hull construction using a number of planks laminated together.

BRIDLE.—A short line attached at two points to tether a model for running.

BRIG.—A two masted square-rigged vessel.

BRIGANTINE.—A two masted vessel square-rigged on the foremast, and fore and aft rigged on the main.

BULKHEAD.—An internal solid frame dividing the ship.

BULLSEYE.—A circular block grooved round its edge, and pierced through the centre for ropes.

BULWARK.—The sides of the vessel above deck level.

BUNT.—The centre of the square sail.

BUSH.—A metal bearing.

CABLE LAID.—A rope in which the strands run to the left.

CAM.—A rotating disc bearing against an arm, and shaped so that the arm is raised or lowered at certain points of rotation.

CAMBER.—The thwartship curve of a deck.

CAPSTAN.—A drum revolving vertically, used for hauling in a rope, etc.

CARAVEL.—A three masted vessel similar to a galleon, but considerably smaller.

CATALYST.—A chemical reagent which when mixed with other materials starts an irreversible chemical change.

CENTREBOARD.—The fin keel which can be raised or lowered in a well to provide additional side area for shallow draft boats.

CENTRE OF GRAVITY.—The point through which the weight of the boat may be said to act.

CHAIN PIPE.—A casting set in the deck through which the anchor chain passes into the chain locker.

CHAIN PLATE.—A fitting for the attachment of the main mast shrouds at their lower ends.

CHAMFER.—An angle planed into a piece of timber, out of square with the main faces.

CHINE.—The line where the sides of the boat meet the bottom, forming a sharp angle.

CLEAT.—A fitting with two horns for making fast a rope.

CLEW.—The lower corner of a square sail, or the aft corner of a fore and aft sail.

CLINCHER BUILT.—A method of planking where the lower edge of each plank overlaps the upper edge of the plank below.

CLIPPER.—A three or four mast square-rig vessel employing a very narrow beam hull.

COAMING.—A raised structure round a hatchway or cockpit to prevent water entering.

COMPANIONWAY.—A stairway leading down from the main deck.

COMPRESSION IGNITION.—A type of internal combustion engine in which combustion is effected by the heat generated by compression of the gases.

CONVECTION COOLING.—A method of cooling an engine by means of a water header tank.

employing the natural tendency of warmed water to rise, thus producing circulation.

COUNTER.—The overhang of the stern.

COURSE.—The main sail on a square-rigged mast.

CRINGLE.—A loop of rope spliced into the edge of a sail.

CROSSJACK.—The lowest yard on the mizzen mast.

CROSS-TREES.—Light timbers to spread the rigging of a mast.

CROSS-SECTION.—A true section of a hull, etc., at any point looking along the longitudinal axis.

CUTWATER.—The part of the stem on the actual water line.

CUTTER.—Formerly a single masted vessel carrying a square sail and a boom mainsail, topsail and gaff topsail ; nowadays normally fore and aft rigged.

DAVIT.—A type of small crane for hoisting and lowering ships boats.

DEADEYE.—A wooden block grooved round the periphery, and equipped with three holes to pass ropes.

DEADRISE.—The angle of a ship's bottom from the horizontal.

DEADWOOD.—Normally the solid wood part of a keel.

DECK PIPE.—The upper lip of the anchor hawse pipes.

DISPLACEMENT.—The weight of the volume of water displaced by a boat, i.e. the weight of the boat itself.

DRAFT (Draught).—The distance between the waterline and the lowest point of the keel.

DOWEL.—Timber, usually birch, purchased in strips of circular section.

EARING.—A rope used in bending a sail, particularly at the corners of a square sail.

EGG-BOX CONSTRUCTION.—A method of building where structural members are all halved together.

EYEBOLT.—A bolt with a loose ring in its head.

EYEPLATE.—A small plate incorporating an eye used in securing or passing a line.

FAIRLEAD.—A fitting for guiding a rope.

FALL.—A rope which with blocks comprises a tackle, e.g. boat falls as fitted to davits.

FEATHER EDGE.—A timber which is tapered off to a knife edge along one side.

FLANGE.—A rim projecting at right angles.

FLEMISH COIL.—A coil of rope in which each coil lies flat, giving the appearance of a mat.

FLYING JIB.—The outermost headsail.

FOOT-ROPE.—A rope mounted on a square yard on which to stand.

FORE (Forward).—Towards the bow.

FORE AND AFT.—From stem to stern ; along the longitudinal axis.

FORECASTLE.—Space beneath the forward portion of the deck, usually abbreviated to fo'c'sl.

FOREFOOT.—The point where the stem meets the keel.

FOREMAST.—The mast nearest the bow.

FORESAIL.—The largest sail set on the foremast.

FORESTAY.—A stay running down from the mast, and made to brace the mast against backward stresses.

FRAME.—A thwartship structural member of the hull.

FULCRUM.—The point about which rotation takes place.

FURL.—To bunch up and secure sails.

FUTTOCK.—A portion of a frame ; in a ship each frame usually comprises six to eight futtocks.

GAFF.—A spar on the afterside of the mast supporting the head of a fore and aft sail.

GAFF TOPSAIL.—A triangular sail filling in the space between the gaff and the top mast.

GALLEON.—15th, 16th or 17th century sailing vessel, notable for a high poop.

GALLOWS FRAME.—Framework carrying a platform for stowing boats, etc., above deck level.

GANGWAY.—An opening in the bulwarks.

GANGWAY LADDER (Accommodation Ladder).—Steps leading down the ship's side.

GARBOARD STRAKE.—The plank next to the keel.

GASKET.—A rope wound round the furled sail ; a relatively soft packing piece between two joined surfaces.

GOOSENECK.—A swivel joint by which the heel of a boom is held to the mast.

GOVERNOR.—A mechanism fitted to some motors to limit the maximum speed.

GUDGEON.—An eye in which a rudder pintle turns.

GUNWALE.—The top-most edge of the deck, or a small boat rail.

GUY.—A line used to steady a spar.

GUYING.—Carrying out a gye.

GYBE.—A change of course relative to the wind when running, with the main boom swinging to the opposite side.

GYE.—To change tack intentionally when sailing to windward ; also the mechanism used to change tack.

HALLIARD (Halyard).—The rope used to hoist sails or yards, etc.

HATCH.—An opening for the deck ; the cover for such an opening.

HAWSE PIPE.—The pipe emerging in the side of the bow through which the anchor chain passes.

HAWSER.—A heavy rope.

HAWSER LAID.—A rope in which the strands run to the right.

HEAD.—The top or outboard end, e.g. mast head, etc. ; the top side or corner of a sail.

HEADSAILS.—Fore and aft sails forward of the foremast.

HEEL.—The bottom or inboard end, e.g. mast heel ; the canted angle at which a vessel sails.

HELM.—The tiller or steering mechanism.

HOUNDS.—A mast fitting carrying cross trees, etc.

HORSE.—A thwartship rail to which a model's sheets are hooked.

IDLER GEAR.—A small gear doing no work, but reversing the rotation of a second gear.

INTERNAL COMBUSTION ENGINE.—Any engine deriving its power from the expansion of gases burned internally.

IRONS.—"In irons"—when a boat comes up into wind and will not pay off, she is in irons. The condition is accompanied by sail-shaking, etc.

JACK LINE.—A taut line on which a sail is bent.

JAWS.—A type of wooden crutch at the heel of a boom engaging the mast.

JIB.—A triangular sail set on a stay forward of the mast.

JIB BOOM.—A spar extending beyond the bowsprit ; the spar attached to the foot of a model yacht jib.

JIG.—An internal or external structural member, assuring accurate alignment.

JIGGER.—A small fore and aft sail on the after mast of a yawl, etc.

JOGGLING.—The irregular jointing of deck planks into a kingplank or other plank running in a different direction.

JUMPER STRUT.—A strut used to extend a backstay.

KEDGE.—A type of light anchor.

KEEL.—The backbone of a vessel.

KEELSON.—The heavy timber fitted to the keel for reinforcement.

KETCH.—A two masted vessel with a small after mast stepped forward of the rudder post.

KILN-DRYING.—A process of baking timber in a kiln to dry off sap.

KINGPLANK.—The central plank of the deck running fore and aft.

KITCHIN RUDDER.—A device consisting of two cups fitting round the propeller, and adjustable for steering or for speed control and movement astern.

LAMINATE.—To build up in several layers bonded together.

LANYARD.—A light rope for making anything fast.

LARBOARD.—Disused term for port side.

LATEEN.—A large triangular sail set at an angle to the mast.

LEACH.—The after edge of a fore and aft sail ; the sides of a square sail.

LIFT.—A rope attached to the end of a spar supporting its weight and determining its vertical position.

LIVERPOOL BOY.—A light rubber band on an adjustable line, attached to a jib-boom and tending to keep the jib on one tack.

LOOF.—That part of a ship where the beam narrows towards the stern.

LUFF.—The forward edge of a fore and aft sail ; to allow a vessel to come up to the wind.

MAIN MAST.—The middle of a three masted vessel, or after mast of a two master, except a yawl or ketch where it is the forward mast.

MAINSAIL.—The largest sail on the main mast.

MIZZEN MAST.—The after mast.

MOCK-UP.—To make a dummy non-working model in the same size as the finished prototype.

O.D.—Outside Diameter. (I.D. is inside diameter.)

PARREL.—A band or strap securing a yard to a mast, but allowing the yard to be moved up and down.

PAWL.—A pivoted lever engaging in pockets in a wheel, preventing the wheel from moving back.

PAY OFF.—To turn away from the wind.

PEAK.—The tip of a gaff, or the corner of a sail attached thereto ; the speed of which maximum power is produced by an engine.

PINTLE.—The pin fitted to a rudder to provide a hinge movement.

PLATE AND BULB.—A keel consisting of a thin plate, swelling out at the bottom for the lead.

POOP.—The raised deck at the after end of the vessel ; in the navy, the quarter deck.

PORT.—The left-hand side of a ship ; an opening in the side of a hull or deck.

QUADRANT.—A segment of a circle ; a navigational instrument.

QUARTER.—The side of the vessel between stern and the attachment point of the after rigging.

RAKE.—The angle of the mast from the vertical, the angle of the stem or transom.

RATLINE.—Small ropes passing across shrouds to form a ladder.

REEF.—To reduce sail area.

REEVE.—To run a line through a hole.

RESIN BONDED.—Glued together by means of a water and heat proof resin glue.

RIB AND PLANK.—A hull built by planking on to ribs which remain part of the finished structure.

ROUND BILGE.—A boat in which turn of the bilge is a continual curve.

RUBBING STRAKE (Rubber).—A fore and aft timber laid externally to protect the planking.

RUNNING LIGHTS (Steaming Lights).—Lights carried on each side of a vessel in motion, red to port and green to starboard.

RUNNING RIGGING.—Lines for setting sails etc., which are moved from time to time, standing rigging is the permanent bracing, etc. for masts.

SCARF.—A joint between two pieces of timber, blending them into one.

SCHNORKEL.—A device which can be surfaced by a submerged submarine, through which air may be drawn into the boat.

SCHOONER.—A fore and aft rigged vessel with anything from two to seven masts. A topsail schooner is two masted carrying a square top and top gallant sail on the fore.

SEIZE.—To bind with light cord.

SCUPPER.—A drain cut through a bulwark.

SELVEDGE.—The manufactured edge of cloth.

SHACKLE.—A U-shaped iron fitting with a pin closing the open end.

SHARPIE.—A hard chine boat.

SHEAVE.—The grooved wheel in a block.

SHEER.—The curve of a deck viewed from abeam; the concavity of the sides or bottom.

SHEET.—The rope attached to the clew of a sail.

SHIP.—Strictly a three or four mast vessel, square-rigged on all masts.

SHOCK MOUNTING.—Mounting on rubber, etc., so that vibration, etc., is not transmitted to the fitting.

SIGNAL GENERATOR.—A piece of wireless apparatus, comparison with which enables a transmitter's frequency to be determined.

SKIN.—The covering of planking forming the sides and bottom of the hull.

SKYLIGHT.—A window over a cabin, etc.

SLOOP.—A single masted fore and aft rigged vessel.

SOLENOID.—An iron core which is withdrawn into a wire coil when the coil is electrically energised.

SPANKER.—The fore and aft sail on the mizzen mast.

SPAR.—A yard, gaff or boom.

SPINNAKER.—A large triangular sail set on a

boom on the opposite side of the mast to the main boom, and used when running.

SPREADER.—A strut extending from the crosstrees to spread the backstays.

SPRITSAIL.—A square sail set beneath the bowsprit.

SQUARE-RIGGED.—Equipped with square sails the yards of which are thwartship.

STANCHION.—The vertical pillars carrying rails.

STARBOARD.—The right side of the boat looking forward.

STAY.—A heavy rope used to brace a mast.

STEM.—The foremost timber in a hull.

STERN.—The after end of a ship.

STERN POST.—A vertical timber joined to the after end.

STERN SHEETS.—The space in the stern of the small boat.

STRAKE.—A plank running the length of the hull.

STRINGER.—A light structural member running fore and aft.

STROPPING.—Encircling a block with a rope.

STUFFING BOX.—A short bearing through which a propeller shaft emerges from the hull.

SUPERSTRUCTURE.—The part of a boat above deck level.

SWEAT.—To run solder through a joint by means of a blowlamp, etc.

TACK.—The lower forward corner of a fore and aft sail ; the rope that holds down the forward clew of a square sail when on the wind ; to sail into wind.

TACKLE.—Gear composed of blocks and rope.

TAFFRAIL.—A rail round the stern.

TEMPLATE.—A pattern cut to check the shape.

THROAT.—The forward upper corner of the fore and aft sail.

THWART.—A small boat seat.

THWARTSHIP.—From side to side.

TILLER.—A bar connected to the rudder head and moved from side to side.

TIMBERHEAD.—Part of the frame projecting above deck against which the bulwarks are built.

TOP HAMPER.—The rigging, etc., above deck.

TOPPING LIFT.—A tackle holding up the end of a boom or yard.

TOPSIDES.—The sides of the hull above the waterline.

TRANSOM.—The flat, usually upright, stern of a boat.

TRAVELLER.—A ring or pulley sliding across a horse.

TUMBLEHOME.—The inward slope of the topsides.

TURNBUCKLE.—A screw device for tightening rigging.

VANE GEAR.—A device used to steer a model at a constant angle to the wind.

VANG.—A rope steadying the outer end of a gaff.

WAIST.—The mid portion of the deck.

WALE.—A heavy strake running fore and aft.

WATERLINE.—The line at which a vessel rides when afloat.

WATERWAY.—A channel running round the deck serving as a gutter.

WEAR.—To change tack while running.

WHIP.—A single block fitted with a line ; the springiness natural to timber, etc.

WINCH.—An engine fitted with a drum for holding a rope.

WINDLASS.—A mechanical device for hoisting an anchor.

WORM.—To lay thin twine between the strands of a rope to present a smooth surface ; a gear used when considerable reduction in speed is required.

XEBEC.—Lateen rigged Mediterranean vessel.

YARD.—A horizontal spar from which a square sail is set.

YARD ARM.—The outer eighth of a yard.

YAWL.—A fore and aft rig consisting of two masts, the after one being very small and stepped behind the sternpost.

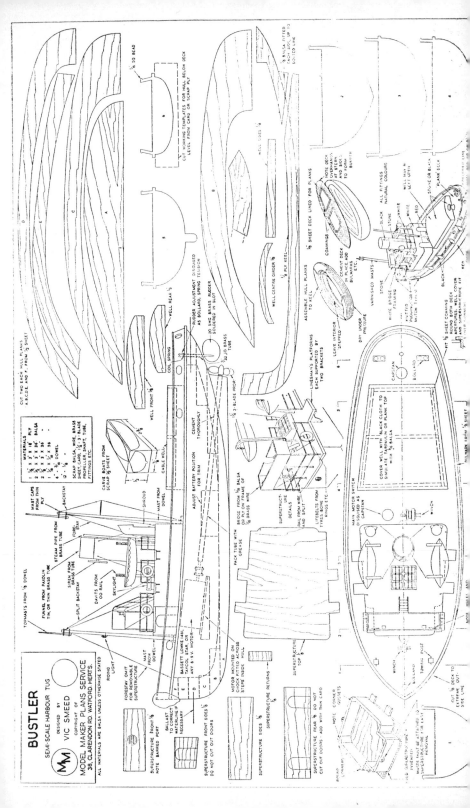

BUSTLER

SEMI-SCALE HARBOUR TUG

DESIGNED BY

VIC SMEED

COPYRIGHT OF

MODEL MAKER PLANS SERVICE

38 CLARENDON RD WATFORD HERTS.

ALL MATERIALS ARE BALSA UNLESS OTHERWISE STATED